Controversial Expectations

The Life Tutor Without a Face

Wynie A van Wyngaarden

authorHOUSE®

AuthorHouse™ UK Ltd.
1663 Liberty Drive
Bloomington, IN 47403 USA
www.authorhouse.co.uk
Phone: 0800.197.4150

Published by AuthorHouse 05/09/2014

ISBN: 978-1-4969-8026-7 (sc)
ISBN: 978-1-4969-8029-8 (hc)
ISBN: 978-1-4969-8027-4 (e)

Contents

ACKNOWLEDGMENT

This book is dedicated to all the many ex-wives, ex-husbands,

ex-partners and friends.

Who opened their hearts, shared their feelings,

hardships and their experiences.

Moreover, those people I have discovered whom do not live to pretend.

"If I was perfect, what would I need?"

"If I was imperfect, what would I need?"

and

"If I had to live my love . . .

. . . wounded I have lived my life?"

Wynie

1

Someday . . . I would understand

Strolling down the road one warm summer's day in my hometown of Johannesburg, South Africa, with bow and arrows in hand, a tie around my head, and a chicken feather or two wedged between the tie and my ear, I felt like the Big Chief himself, especially after happily hunting my feathers in the back yard of the local English and music teacher.

With chickens scattered all over the place, and the cock close on my heels, I had gotten my feathers and had made it over the fence just in time. Old Mrs Grease's sharp, piercing voice was more than enough to remove anyone swiftly from her property.

Yes! I made it! I was not Big Chief himself, but I was out hunting with him—and the buffalo were many. He was teaching me how to shoot and use my bow and arrow. I was just aiming and ready to release the arrow to find its target when my imagination was interrupted. 'What are you doing? What are you shooting?'

He was very old. My eyes grew larger as I noticed all the lines on his face. He was smiling, and his face was friendly. He did not seem like an enemy.

All the wrinkles next to the corners of his mouth and around his nose and eyes, as well as on his forehead, just under his hat, were deep. The dark pupils of his eyes were highlighted with the surrounding white. What arrested my attention was his sad and tired look. I stepped back.

'So! What are you doing, boy?' he said in friendly manner.

'I'm shooting big buffalo. I am on the hunt!' I replied with great confidence.

'Where do you come from, hunter, and what is your name?' he asked with a smile as he sat down on the pavement, lifting his hat slightly higher. His eyes had the 'hunter' wondering about him, and I kept my distance.

'I am playing. I live in the corner house, and my name is Alwyn. Why?'

When the elderly man uttered, 'I did not come to declare war,' I noticed some of his teeth were missing.

'Oh, did your teeth not grow back?' I asked him. 'Is that why you look so sad?'

At first, he smiled and looked around as if he wondered if anyone had heard us. He took his hat off and rolled it between the palms of his hands. He did it in the same way that Dad rolled a newspaper when he wanted to spank my younger brother or chase the dogs out of the house. Then he turned to me, lifting his head while placing his hat back on his head and biting his bottom lip. 'Yes, I do have sad eyes, people tell me. I always wanted a child, but I had a disease as a child. Now, no boy will ever call me Daddy.'

He had a tear in his eye, and he started to walk away. He then turned around after a while and said, 'You must let the cowboys teach you how to shoot.'

'*Nooo!*' I called out. 'The cowboys shoot Indians! *No!*'

'Good to hear. Never shoot.' He bent down to my 'hunter's' height. 'Never hate people, and always be yourself.' He walked on, did not turn around again, and disappeared.

Where that man went, no one will ever know. What I did know was that I was six years old and very unhappy about the fact that the movies showed the cowboys as heroes for shooting Indians.

That man looked like an old Indian hunter who had lost his tribe. Like the Lion King who had lost his leadership. Like the football player who had lost his position on the team before he could retire in dignity. Even a mother who had lost her child would have shown sympathy and grace.

I informed my father about the old man. I was crying. Dad reminded me not to speak to strangers. He told me that someday I would understand what the old man had tried to say. 'You will grow up one day. End of discussion.'

Are not the tomorrows of life an untried path for the young—even unto the aged? —Wynie

2

Two for the price of one

Diagonally across the road, down the street, in a semi-detached house, lived a Lebanese family with nine children. I was the eldest child in my own family, and I was friends with their youngest children.

One Saturday I was invited to their home for their movie evening. My father was a difficult man; he did not want me to go unless John, my younger brother, tagged along. That normally meant trouble for me, so I refused to go.

Uncle Peter, the uncle of these nine children, was a very friendly Lebanese. When I refused his invitation, he came to our house, knocked on our door, and asked Dad why I would refuse to join a lovely 'get together'. With his hands on his hips he looked up at my father and said, 'Now tell this "Leb" to his face!'

Father tried to give a good reason for wanting my younger brother to go with me: 'What's good for the one is good for the other,' he said.

Uncle Peter then, in soft voice, cleared the air by saying, 'Honestly now, who of your bothers was not a pain in the butt when you were this age?' My dad was lost for words.

'Mr Van,' said Uncle Peter, 'may you enjoy your evening.' And off he went.

At the age of about seven, I never thought anyone would talk to my father in such a manner and get away with it.

'Yes!' Father allowed me to go as Uncle Peter retreated. 'Tell that old man that, if I did not like him so much, I would have broken his jaw!'

He said this just loud enough for everyone to hear as I closed the door behind me.

I was always welcomed by Uncle Peter as 'Drina's child.'

'My name is Alwyn, not Drina's child.'

'Alwyn, you are very welcome here, but I have news for you. You will always be Drina's child.' Uncle Peter smiled.

There I was waiting for the projector to start rolling; the action would soon be on a big white sheet. The smell of popcorn coming from the kitchen was irresistible, and the big bowl made its rounds. I knew that, by the time it was my turn, there would be only small bits of overly salty popcorn left.

Then just in time, Uncle Peter's wife saved the moment. '*Shame* Lucy, fill up that dish so that everyone will get enough.' I assure you, more than enough corn was popping out of that kitchen.

Zorba the Greek was the adults' first choice, and everybody's spirit lifted. The Greek visitors joined in clapping hands and singing, so everyone clapped with them, lifting the spirits even higher. (Not to mention the alcoholic spirits that had been mixed into the Coca Cola.)

At the end of *Zorba*, everyone was waiting in anticipation for the next action movie to begin. For a little boxer like me, action was welcome.

'Ten . . . nine . . . eight,' all eyes on that big white sheet. 'Three . . . two . . . one . . . *Action!*' This was the welcoming chant.

Horses, guns, cigarettes, and alcohol . . . cowboys were standing around in the hills planning their bounty hunt and loading their rifles. As an Indian family was passing by below their perch. A cowboy up on the mountain took aim, shot, and the Indian dropped off his horse.

I jumped up in despair over the cowboys shooting Indians again. Everyone seemed okay with it. I was not. All eyes were on me by now. Not only was I in the minority, but I had been the only fool willing to express my feelings.

I made my way home after the film broke and the projector stopped. I was distressed. *Why must the cowboys shoot the Indians? Why!*

When I ran down the passage, making my way to the front door, I had to put on brakes. Big granddad stood there waiting. 'You're upset, young man. Come here and tell me why you are so unhappy.'

I told him and gave him my opinion about it all.

Big granddad, the eldest person in my friend's home, sat down on the couch. He looked at my hands, then reached out and took them in his old hands. 'You can box,' he began. 'I have seen you draw blood from other boys' noses, but you are upset about what you see in the movie.' His big nose drew my attention, and his heavy breathing made the words come out bit by bit.

I asked him if he was sick. 'No! However, I am old and want to tell you not to get upset about what you see in a movie. It's only the acting out of a story. It is not real blood, my boy.'

I pulled my hands out of his. 'My father said the Indians live in America, and the cowboys live there, so it's real.'

'It is history, and they do not live like that anymore,' he went on. 'They live like the Indians on the other side of Hannover Avenue.' He was attempting to calm me down.

I arrived home. Beer bottles were on the table again. Mom did not seem happy. 'Are you fighting again?' I asked.

Mom just nodded her head, and I turned to walk out.

'This son of yours,' said my father to my mother, 'why must he always be so different? He's not my son!'

I heard that and turned around . . . 'I am glad you're not my dad, because my dad would not drink like this.'

Well, no need to explain what happened next: 'I'm your father!' he asserted in the highest tone of voice, 'and you better believe that!' Just like him. 'End of discussion.'

'The Indians live like those on the other side of Hannover Avenue.' My friends' granddad's words were on my mind. I had to go and see for myself.

My memory takes me to a time when I went with Mom when she went to buy wool and other materials. Buying raw materials and making one's own clothes had a good influence on one's budget.

If my memory serves me right, in the manner it should, my brother and one of my three sisters went with us.

We entered Indian Territory, but there were no buffalo; the closest thing with four legs other than a horse was an occasional cat or dog. The Indians had my attention. This side of Hannover Avenue was a familiar sight; I had been here before. Everywhere there were cries of 'Good price, madam!' 'Two for the price one, madam!'

In one of the shops we entered, I noticed a human being totally dressed in black linen. I noticed the white of the eyes first, and then the dark eyes moved. That was no Red Indian in black clothes! What I saw here did not match up with the movies, even though the cowboys went to Indian Territory to buy goods from them.

What was going on?

This expedition though the Asian town was a revelation. As we were strolling on, a sales transaction captured my attention. The Indian stood next to his black African client, both facing the mirror as the client's friend sat to the side. The client was trying on a suit for size. A big smile on his face showed a happy mood as he stood upright and proud, his expectations obviously exceeded by far. Suddenly the mood changed. His friend stood up and pushed the Indian aside abruptly.

The verbal language I did not understand, but the body language was evident. He accused the salesperson of disguising the baggy backside of the pants. The Indian pretended that he did not know what they were complaining about.

'Two for the price of one!' often echoed in my ears. It did not sound right. My introduction to business had me confused. One loaf of bread cost five cents. One pint of milk cost seven cents. Was someone cheating? I could not say why, but the Indians disappointed me.

Is the human mind not endowed with the capacity to discriminate?
—*Wynie*

3

Emphasizing the facts

Have you ever played soccer in the streets? Tested ball sense with a tennis ball? Used 750-millilitre Sprite, Coke, Fanta, and Pepsi bottles as goalposts?

Four a side, Lusitania verses Rangers, Pommies against the Portuguese, and imported players of all cultures. Tar road, bare feet—some with shoes—and the touchline was the edge of the pavement. Rangers from south to north, downhill, and Lusitania from north to south, uphill, and there were no goalkeepers, as it was the defenders' job to prevent scoring.

Fifteen minutes after kick-off the match was in full swing. We moved like lightning, passing the ball, dribbling, and stepping on the ball with rolling spins. Our team was doing well. I was one of Lusitania's import players, and the defender had me looking after the goalposts.

Just before halftime, Lusitania's goalposts were under attack. As I ran downhill to defend the posts, which were about a metre apart, I heard such a horrifying sound. The sound so distracted me that the opposition scored a goal against us. I turned around, and my ear traced the sound to my friend Alfonso's house. 'Alfonso, those sounds come from your home,' I called.

'No, man, it can't be,' he said, and he called for play to continue.

Now I heard the sound of a pig in distress. I listened to the tone, the frequency indicating an urgency to escape. Then the sound faded momentarily without hope that some sort of grace would be in time to save the day. There was nothing but eternal hush.

Suddenly, the squealing resumed and pierced my ears. Alfonso ran up to me with unaccustomed speed and stopped me in time from looking over the solid, precast wall. 'They are slaughtering a pig.' His eyes were like saucers. 'Don't look at what's happening there. Let's play ball. Please?' And he dragged me away.

'Why don't they do it at the abattoir? Why in your backyard? Why?'

'My dad says it is cheaper,' he justified. 'He saves money for other stuff we need.'

That day, I was not a good goal defender, and the result was as usual: the four winners received the drink bottles as prize money. It was well spent on sweets, as the deposit refund was worth a few cents.

Slaughtering at home to save money was a controversial incident in my young mind. For days on end, Alfonso's dad was under my 'eagle's eye'. He became something from another planet in my opinion. Alfonso was embarrassed for his parents' sake, and avoided playing. The probing questions concerning the digested pig forced him into hiding.

Factory workers, who had been working overtime, walked up Fifteenth Avenue out of Church Street, passed our corner house, and continued left into Clifton Street. It was here where fear of snakes became a big event for me. It looked like a snake—rags stuffed into the leg of a stocking, tied off with gut at the one end. At about ten meters, the men noticed something moving. From behind the tree, I pulled the string to move the demonic creature that was so near to the pedestrians' path.

Then one worker spotted a meter or so from the dangerous, cold-blooded creature. Fear kicked in, and the terror of the mamba's 'lethal strike' had his adrenalin turbo charged. His two legs motored at a speed that would make Usain Bolt—Jamaican sprinter, 'the fastest person ever'—look like he was taking a casual afternoon stroll.

As if he was not moving fast enough, the neighbourhood fox terrier directed her canines to his heels. Our enjoyment of that moment was priceless, for Hollywood would have paid a small fortune to capture the action!

Finally, the terrified worker returned, stick in hand, in search of the snake, only to find two youngsters with big smiles on their faces. He nodded his head and returned the smile. 'You won't catch me again,' said the man with the big ring in his ear.

'Zulu Chief! I am up for the challenge! Catch you later!' I dared

Zulu Chief smiled, showing his Colgate teeth, and said, '*Suka wena*,' and ran off.

Five o'clock in the afternoon, a week or so later. The plan with the same 'snake' was ready for execution, but from another angle. We had to put our patience on ice, as Zulu Chief was nowhere to be seen.

Suddenly there were a few shots from across the road, from the direction of the 'pig slaughtering station'. I realized it had come from inside Alfonso's house.

Then there was a male voice shouting in a foreign language and then another 'bang'! The man in there was on a mission. More shouts and yet another 'bang'!

A deadly silence settled over the western front. I was absolutely certain in my mind that the voices of that home had been silenced in a manner beyond my healthy imagination.

Using more guts than brains, I approached the house with my head well below the wall. I opened the gate silently and hurried to a corner were nobody might notice my presence. With my back to the wall, I moved slowly towards the window where I might just have a glimpse of evidence lying on the floor—a wall that might bear evidence of a bullet's invasion, or even the intruder himself.

From my angle of observation, I noticed through the ribbed, see-through glass Alfonso's silhouette holding an object in his hand. Was that a gun? Had he shot his father? His father may have been cruel to them. Had Alfonso had to stop his dad? I watched Alfonso put the object to his face. I had to stop him!

I jumped to the window and knocked nervously to draw Alfonso's attention and to save my friend from himself.

Then the door opened. The questions tumbled out of my mouth: 'Are you okay? Where is the gun? Who shot who?'

Alfonso looked surprised and did not answer until just after swallowing what he was chewing. 'There were no guns and no shooting here.' He then took another bite of the toasted cheese and tomato.

'I heard a few gunshots in this house,' I insisted.

'Hey, Alfonso . . .' his father called in their foreign language.

'My dad said you must come in. They're in the kitchen.'

I walked into the kitchen. There was no one wounded or dead; all were still alive. The mother stood at the washbasin with a cup of tea in hand, and the father sat at the table, wine in hand, finishing the last of his supper. Alfonso was busy with the other half of his toasted cheese and tomato. All seemed normal.

'What happened here? Who shot who?' I had to know.

Alfonso was the messenger, interpreter, and deliverer. As he explained my concerns to his father, smiles lit up the faces of father and son. The mother's face stayed without expression.

'My dad says you need to have some table wine like a good Portuguese, and relax,' my friend told me.

I needed to know, 'Who was shooting?'

Alfonso walked up to the table with hands in the air like a preacher blessing the congregation. He moved them in a 'please be seated' gesture towards me. The velocity of those hands increased, as if powered by a compressor. 'My father said he was only talking to my mother, "emphasizing" with a *bang!*' He demonstrated, and the big table jumped around. 'Only emphasizing the facts,' he boastfully concluded.

Alfonso's mother turned to us, her emotional mood of rebellion ignited. She gave Alfonso a grin, and his dad the 'disgustful' eye. 'It is good when my husband is strong,' she said. 'I like him strong . . . but talking so ugly to me . . . *is wrong!*'

How often does one seek expression of one's conviction? —*Wynie*

4

Appetite controls individuals' behaviour

At the age of eleven, I started working in a fish and chips shop. The Boy Scouts had me taking part in Bob-a-Job week. During this yearly event, scouts go round the village doing jobs for a bob (a bob used to be a shilling; now it's five pence). My mother's words, 'If you don't ask, you may never receive' were a pain in the butt until the day I stopped in front of the counter at the Greek man's store, looked him in the eye, and very bravely said, 'I'd like a chocolate please.'

'Have you made your choice?' he asked.

'I don't have money.'

'*Neh*, you don't have money.' His words flowed from his lips and landed harshly on my ears.

'Yes, I don't have money, but I will do some work for you to pay for it. I'll even sweep the floor for it.'

The owner's eyes nearly popped out of their sockets. His upper and bottom lips parted, leaving a big gap as his jaw dropped. Two to three seconds felt like ages.

Then, 'Let me think about it,' he said, and he turned to serve his paying customers.

After many customers left he said, 'You are still here. Your mother will kill me if I make you work here.'

'No! She won't mind! It's Boy Scout Bob-a-Job week, see?' I said determinedly.

He shook his head and walked off, just to return with a broom in hand. From that day on, I worked for a number of owners at the same shop, over a number of years—an education in its own right.

Every day was a new experience; everyday happenings were like a play on stage—drama, comedy, or thriller.

Each lunch-hour rush was a mission of its own: preparing beforehand and then cutting, slicing, packing, and weighing. When we heard the factory sirens from far away, we knew the factory workers would be arriving in a little while. Soon the doors would be stormed with hungry faces. They did not buy only Coke and smokes. I was bombarded by a chorus of requests, needs, and demands, for their appetites controlled their individual tastes: 'Five cents butter, two slices, and ten cents liver spread!' 'Half white, half brown.' 'Chips, two Vienna's, and a half loaf of bread . . . I do not want brown . . . I want a white bread.' The crowd's demands continued.

At one point, a customer placed a box on the counter. It was a tall order, amounting to far more items than were usually purchased by a customer in our store.

'Is your attention drawn away from us?' another customer asked.

'The box is not talking to you. It has nothing to say. I am human, not a box. I pay,' someone else playfully said.

'Come . . . come . . .' from yet another. 'We are in a hurry and want to eat. We don't have all day.' They were all pressing for speedier service.

The owner spoke up: 'Oh, your mouth is big today and—'

'Yes! Of course,' the client interrupted. 'That is why I am in your shop—to stuff food inside of it, so it can go quiet.'

Then George, the owner, had a solution. 'You may get my boot down your mouth—'

'Oh, that's okay. I am so hungry I could just eat it,' the big man in the overall responded.

'*Wena!*' (You!) 'I have only two hands, two feet, two ears, and two eyes . . . one nose and one mouth. I am not Superman!'

The customer dressed in the blue overall placed his hand under his chin and smiled. 'Hey—that is good. I am happy to hear you are normal!' The crowd just loved it.

There were many different faces; some showed impatience, others haste. There were those who were soft spoken, and many who were loud boasters and demand more than was required. Thank goodness for the ones who smiled and offered a 'please' and 'thank you'; they made it all worthwhile.

A couple walked in holding hands, bringing in cheerfulness and joy as they giggled and flirted and hugged and kissed. They stepped in unison up to the fridge and took out Cokes, and then the naughty 'chick' needed a smoke. He then took out his wallet, paid for the drink, and asked for change to play pinball.

She obviously detested his decision to play pinball; it seemed that time was of the essence. He paid her no mind, just combed his hair and chewed gum with nothing to say until he reached the end of the game.

'Giggle' and 'Flirt' were then nowhere in evidence; 'cheerful' and 'joy' were replaced by thunder and hate.

At that moment, their 'need to love' turned into 'love to hate', and all the good went out of the gate.

He kicked the pinball machine for beating him that day.

Surely, his 'doll' had to assume he did not mean it that way, and her sulk did not last, for in him she had the best catch.

What did she expect? That a man would dance to her song? Never.

Does appetite not bear influence, even unto the powerful? —Wynie

5

No redeemer anywhere

Now the English, citizens of that very old nation somewhere on an island where there is little sun, witnessed many proud citizens leave their shores.

Depressed by the cloudy weather and cold, they found at the pub a glass of something to break the chill. They received the magic of crystal liquid gold, which warmed the blood, the feelings, and the emotions . . . and made them proud.

Many an English family moved into our suburbs. Many of their comments always had me wonder where they would like to be, however interesting . . .

- 'Me dad worked for the British navy. He made our soldiers good food with English gravy.'
- 'Hello Mrs Van how are you? The weather is good—far better than in London today.'
- 'Me mom was not happy with me choice of husband and the type of father he might become. So, we fled to Africa in fear of me father.'
- 'The English are world conquerors—our royalty, our loyalty, and our courage got us everywhere, and the sun never sets on the British Empire.'
- 'You ask me why we don't return to England. Me wife longs for her family very much, but the cloudy weather had her depressed last time we went back home to Liverpool.'

- 'Back home many men are engineers, you know—plumbing engineers, brick laying engineers, wiring engineers, and garbage engineers.'

My father's sarcasm peaked at this, him being a boilermaker. 'I am a fabrication engineer,' he once said. 'Because they stood near an engine, now they are engineers. In South Africa we should call the mineworkers digging engineers, earth removal engineers, and cave creating engineers. We could call the politicians manipulating engineers, and the bank managers, money mechanics, for they tune the financial carburettor of human livelihood. And the English could be called their project managers.

Our corner house was surrounded by the English: at the west end was Old Mrs Grease, an English and music teacher; at the north end was Mr Moore, an imported 'engineer' and his childless wife. Further up the road, in the direction of the 'sunrise end', yet another English family.

The English navy kitchen commanders' son was swinging on my mother's gas stove, trying to get a glimpse of what was in the pots.

'Aunty Drina . . . what do you have in those pots! What are you making to eat? Wow, it smells good, Aunty Drina.'

There were normally five children around our six-by-three table; this time there were six children, all waiting for what the nostrils suggested would be a delicious meal. Our eyes were on the dishes for various reasons.

'First we will dish up for the visitor.' Mom served, and the young English boy's mouth watered; he did not wait on permission to eat.

'Our royal highness, would your mother not be upset with you for eating here when she dishes up your supper? You seem very hungry?'

'No, Aunty Drina, it's just very nice. Can you spare me some more?'

'Most certainly, young man, your request is similar to the requests of the British soldiers in the Anglo-Boer war. No wonder many of them did not want to go home after the war.' She placed a second helping onto his plate.

'Then the English could have been called "joiners" if they had fallen for our food,' I said, bragging about my mother's food. 'Give them good food and you overpower anybody!'

Not being a big flesh eater, I had an ongoing exchange contract with my brother, John, 'Quick, let's swap food before Dad comes.' And John ended up with all the meat.

'How can you give your meat away?' royalty asked.

'Yes,' said John, 'my father will choke Alwyn if he sees him exchanging his meat.' He turned to me. 'Remember the day he was angry and he turned your plate of food upside down?' John reminded.

'Alwyn,' royalty commanded, 'next time you give meat away, send some my way!'

The young English lord's sister then ran into the kitchen from outside. 'Come, Mum is calling,' she told her brother. Then she turned to my mom. 'Me mum will be very upset if she knows he had supper here,' she said.

'You may join your brother next time, me lady,' my mom invited.

'Come let's go!' she said to her brother as she pushed him from behind. 'Supper is waiting!' Her ponytail swung wildly, reflecting the speed with which she left for home.

At the north end of our house was a twelve-foot piece of ground that was bordered by the fence of Mr Moore and his childless wife. There was a six-foot wall running the thirty-six foot distance from the driveway gate to the garage door. The confined space thus formed was the second 'home' field and mainly where the neighbourhood children kicked the tennis ball around.

In August, my birthday arrived providing me the privilege of a 'real' soccer ball. Wow—I did not allow it out of my sight; it was the most precious gift I had received in a long time.

This time the garage door and driveway gate were the perfect place to score those precious goals. John, the irritating brother, interrupted play after half-time, because no captain had chosen him to be on his team's short list. Play could resume only when the ball was taken away from John.

Joy and excitement was the order of play. Goals and near misses were followed by cheers and shouts of 'Yes! Yes!' The competition was at its highest when my irritating brother appeared from nowhere and kicked the ball over the wall.

'Mr Moore, my brother kicked my ball over your wall. May I please have it back please?' I asked. Mr Moore nodded his head without a word and turned back to go into his house. I sensed trouble and ran back home, jumped up onto the wall and onto the garage roof. Mr Moore came out; he had an object in his hand—a pocketknife. He walked in the direction of the ball, which had landed among his plants. 'James Bond' opened his knife and bent down to pick my ball up.

'No! Please do not puncture my ball . . . please . . . please . . . no please . . . *No! No!*' He punctured my ball. 'Why did you do that?' I cried. There was no redeemer anywhere! Where would one find a miracle that could transform the condition of my ball back to what it had been before my heart had been pierced and my streak of joy had been removed.

I ran to Mother in hope of rescuing my day. When she asked our neighbour why he had pierced my ball, Sir Moore denied it and said, 'Your little boy lied. Why do you accuse me—' Then his childless wife started crying. She was disgusted. We could tell by the way Mrs Moore looked at her husband.

'You see, Mom,' I said. 'Aunty Moore knows it's not a lie.' Then 'James Bond' banged the door, to show he did not want to hear more. From behind the cottage door, we could hear no more.

I ran down to the other corner house where Mr Lee from Japan lived. I was crying, my fear, anger, and frustration obvious. From his gate, Mr Lee made his voice heard: 'You angly . . . You must be calm, not put fight in mind.' Mr Lee waved at me to come closer.

'Old man,' I said between sobs. 'He punctured my ball . . . I am going to shoot his windows.'

'Shoot . . . gun?' Mr Lee looked at me with his eyes wide open.

'No, Kettie . . . shoot a stone.' Mr Lee had lost my meaning somewhere between *shoot, gun,* and *stone.*

In exasperation, I explained, demonstrating with my hands: 'You put stone in slingshot, you pull like this, you pull strong and let go one side. Then stone fly like arrow, and stone can break Englishman's windows.'

'Come, come inside,' said Mr Lee. 'Me give you tea and sweets, and you no angly. Angly go way. Come.' Mr Lee led the way into the kitchen where Mrs Lee was working. Mr Lee and his wife spoke in a very gentle way. She smiled. Her eyes were friendly, and she bowed with head and shoulders. She answered her husband with a singing tone that I understood to mean, 'Sure. I understand.' Mr Lee accompanied me into the dining room.

As we sat at the table, Mr Lee asked, 'Where your ball now? You can fix?'

'No can't fix. Ball is not the same.' My head hung down.

'You must not fight in your mind,' he advised. 'Not cry in your mind . . . not hit, shoot, and kick another man. You power is for talk. You word is power and is strong.' He stopped and smiled, yet his face showed strength. His eyes were strongly focused, as if on a mission.

Mrs Lee entered with a small tray, and Mr Lee indicated to the floor pointing at a bamboo carpet. She knelt down and placed the tray in the middle. Mr Lee invited me to be seated on the carpet. 'You drink tea . . . eat sweet . . . you talk me,' he insisted.

'My mother didn't believe me,' I explained. 'Nobody believed that the old man cut my ball.' I was still very upset.

'Your power is for talk,' Mr Lee told me. 'You word is power and is strong. You must use power of talk every day. Talk is same like fire . . . can make food . . . can make hot if cold. Small fire in house make winter better inside house. You must use good fire.'

My confused face encouraged Mr Lee to explain it from another angle. 'Small water is good—you drink water is good . . . you give flower and tree water, they will grow . . . you eat rice; it grow in water . . . water in tea you drink. Big water is too strong and break everything. Same like man if break everything, is cold inside heart.' He placed his fist on his chest. Mr Lee swallowed deeply. 'Big water kill good fire. Old man is big dam water. He stop your fire for play.' Then, after breathing deeply, he said, 'If old man not come out of big water . . . his heart will not come hot.'

Confused, I said. 'Mr Moore is not in water . . .'

Mr Lee realized that both language and youth were problematic. 'Your words must make heart warm for old man. He go feel sorry him puncture you ball. His wife cry. He feel bad inside . . .' Mr Lee put his fist on his chest again.

'He cut my ball,' I protested. 'I want to break his windows.'

'Okay, break window of old man's heart.'

'His heart?' I raised my voice.

'You shoot "friendly stone" in his heart. He will feel bad. "Friendly stone" break the window of old man's heart. You make cold heart warm with "friendly stone", and then his heart can make good fire. You use you mind, same like shoot bow and arrow. "Friendly stone" not kill man. "Friendly stone" make heart healthy.'

'My mother is calling me,' I said, somewhat bewildered. 'You can hear?'

'Yes. You come tomorrow. You and me talk, okay?'

'Okay!' I ran home.

The English navy kitchen commander's son was dancing around my mother's stove once again, and now his mother was there to.

'Drina, what is that?' 'Mother royalty' was asking. 'What is that you're adding to your food?'

'It's salt. Why don't you use salt when cooking? It could be the reason that your food is not being appreciated these days. And you need some spice as well,' my mother added.

As I looked at the food cooking on the gas stove, my mind started working. *Good fire makes food . . . food makes stomach full. Maybe Mr Moore's life was not good—no spice . . . no salt to make his life tasteful. Maybe he spits the bad food of his life on everybody.*

I then ran out the kitchen, down the passage, and down the road. I knocked on Mr Lee's door and shared my thoughts. Mr Lee heard every word of my newfound insight and confirmed it. 'Yes! Because he fights in his mind, he will fight all people. A man who makes war in his mind becomes sick. A man who does not make war in mind is healthy. Same like good food for body.'

Mr Lee put his hands on either side of my face, palms on my cheeks. His fingers gently covered my ears. 'You must make your mind healthy. You must not hear bad words in your mind. You put good things in your mind, and you will make your power strong like big tree.'

He told me to close my eyes. I did . . . 'Now your eyes is closed. You must learn to close your eyes to bad things. You not blind, but must keep your eyes more open for good things.' His words felt like a whispering of wisdom. 'Now go . . . go make peace in your heart.'

20

I opened my eyes as Mr Lee withdrew his hands. I noticed a tear in his strong and friendly eyes. Mr Lee was touched. 'Now go . . . go make peace in your heart.'

'Okay, Mr Lee. Bye! See you, Mr Lee.' And off I ran while Uncle Lee smiled broadly.

From that day on I always looked at the English through renewed eyes . . . and that included all people as well.

Many times I would see Mr Moore in his small garden. I would smile and wave at him in greeting. Mr Moore noticed and always turned his back on me. Mrs Moore on the other hand made me feel special, grateful to me for not shooting the windows of their home. She was a sweet lady.

I always wondered about the tear in Mr Lee's eye.

Why discuss grievances or ponder thereon? Does it not repel one's blessing?
—*Wynie*

6

Pretence

When I was thirteen, my attention was captured by what the older boys and girls were acting out in their lives. Girls 'dressed to kill' were standing outside. Boys were passing by, combing their hair, seeking attention.

By then I was in the habit of watching people and their actions, and gave special attention to how people were communicating with their bodies, rather than just focusing on the words they were using.

I observed the expressions of the eyes, the twitching of eyelids, the flushing of ears. I watched mouths; for example, one girl's jaw dropped, and another girl's teeth crunched. I watched emotional bottom lips sulking. I was in wonderment over the emotions that might be expressed by a bouncing walk that was accompanied by a side-to-side swaying of the hips.

Men and women, boys and girls walked into the shop after a soccer match for Coke, smokes, and gum. Virile young soccer players gave the young ladies the 'attention' they so desired. They seemed to require it even from a known 'testosterone-filled' liar. The swaying of hips and giggles under ovarian drive kept the testosterone hunt alive.

The art of acting remained, even unto the aged.

Serving a customer from behind the counter was an experience I believe most people should have at some stage in their lives.

Customers displayed different moods as they stood right in front of me asking for what they wanted. I would hear the coins drop on the counter, then, 'Twenty Lucky Strike.' The next person would say simply, 'Smokes.

The regular, man.' Yet another would say, 'I need twenty Lexington, please.' So their moods changed day by day.

Human habits reveal human character.

Mr Wilson stopped in his driveway when he came home from work, walked fifty metres to the store for the *Star* newspaper, then walked back home taking four times the length of time, scanning all the headlines by the time he entered his front door.

Every afternoon at about 5:15, he would walk in to the store, take the newspaper from the shelf, and dig into his pocket for his eleven cents. He'd place the money on the counter without taking his eyes off the day's happenings that were revealed on the front page. Clearly he was not happy about what he was reading.

Monday came. Mr Wilson's 5:15 time came and went. I noticed that there was one newspaper left, so I kept it aside for him while I served the other customers.

In the midst of the busy hour, I looked up. There stood a man in pyjamas and slippers, a scarf around his neck. He was red in the face. His eyes were locked in one position as he looked me in the eye. 'How dare you not order enough newspapers? I'm here every day. I'm a regular and you do not have—'

His voice went quiet as I held up the newspaper I had saved for him. He reached for it. 'I kept it aside for you, Mr Wilson.'

The money dropped on the usual place, and without lifting an eye from the headlines, he walked out. All eyes were on him in amazement.

Weighing up the things people did and how people lived was a most wonderful experience—usually. However, sometimes it was *not*.

My high school was some distance from home, and using the bus was awkward for me at times, because sport training and rugby matches kept me from meeting bus departure times. I then had to walk six kilometres to get home.

Transport money tended to be on the opposite side of abundance as well, so I often had to put heel to tar. With school bag on my back, and jacket over my shoulder, I walked home and passed many homes of those kids who were in school with me.

Yes, I would hear, 'Shame he's walking' or 'Did you eat your transport money?' One mother tried to make me feel better: 'At least he is not lazy, and walking will always do anyone good.'

A Deale and Huth Cycles (DHC) ten-speed bicycle was one of my biggest gifts yet. It was old, but I treasured it. Wow! I was a made boy, and I felt as if I belonged to a special group in society. Of course, more than one bike rider, with their many remakes, welcomed me as their friend.

Many afternoons, I would ride home with Alex and Brendan, two brothers. I would sometimes stop at their house. I always admired their furniture, the paintings on the walls, the photos of their holidays.

I once asked, 'If your shoes get too small for you, Alex, do they get passed on to your brother?' I felt like an idiot, because Brendan had a bigger pair of feet than his older brother. They thought it was a joke. For me, well I was weighing up the two households—theirs and mine.

One such an afternoon we raced home. Alex was the first one to arrive, and he noticed the big truck in front of their home. 'What is this?' he asked the repossession man. 'Why are you taking all our stuff?' Then there was a cry from Alex as if he knew what was awaiting the family.

I had seen it more than once at my young age. I said goodbye, but I don't think my word fell upon any ear. As I was getting on my bike, I heard Brendan ask, 'Our bicycles too?'

'They must go as well,' said the man. 'You will get them back when your father can settle his account.'

I went to work. Store owner George the Greek noticed my mood, and he made me tell him what had happened. 'Have a nice cold Coke to calm your nerves. I can't have you serving my customers when you are upset like this.'

That night I did not sleep well. The two brothers had to face everyone at school. My father made me be quiet. He had heard enough. 'Maybe they were trying to live up to the Joneses,' he said surprisingly, in a sympathetic tone of voice.

Next morning I went to school by bus, because I was concerned that my friends might feel unworthy without their bicycles. Just as I got off the bus, they arrived in their mom's motorcar. As we entered the school gates, Alex asked me not to mention what I had seen the previous day; they were embarrassed by what had happened. They were also sure I knew how they felt. 'It must have happened in your home, more than once,' they incorrectly assumed.

Still, I gave my word.

After two to three days, I noticed they started avoiding me. Then the following day, Brendon broke the silence. 'Everybody knows now, thanks to you.' He made it clear that I was not a friend. My newfound friends were lost.

They had to know the truth, and I was going to bring it to the surface. I found out that Lynn, who lived five houses up the road, was with her mother in the car and drove past the truck on that specific day. She confessed that it was her mom who told one of the other mothers. But the truth did not mend my relationship with my friends.

I then tried to speak to their mom. In a friendly way, and yet speaking down to me, she responded, 'Well, as you know, you are not our type after all.' She was smiling as she spoke.

A year or so later, their mother's employer fired her. The charge? Theft.

Is it not in appearance that we override reality—only flattering oneself?
—*Wynie*

7

Headmaster's frustration and Mary Orphan

Just close your eyes for a few seconds. Allow your memory to backtrack, and enjoy a few moments remembering the years you spent at school. You may remember the playground, boys and girls everywhere, trees, plants, and flowers . . . the big sports days and get-togethers when parents contributed to the cheers that motivated the wins and successes of the day or of the past year. Have you been there?

Perhaps you have noticed a young girl walking into the crowd, but no one sees her. Your eyes are drawn to her hair. It is combed, and you know she did her best, for in the orphanage she had to share a comb with the other girls.

'Mary Orphan' needed this outing, for it kept her mind fixed on what she would like in the future. Her sanity, she swore, would be preserved. Every weekend she was allowed to visit her home, as ruled by the magistrate, until her parents rehabilitated. Even at home, it felt as if the walls would collapse. She knew that fresh air would be healthy for mind and emotion.

Mary Orphan walked up to a group of girls. They were all 'dressed to kill'—or in a manner their mothers would approve of, because their dress would show off their social standards. The group took note of her and yet did not see her. The girls grouped up in a bundle and slowly moved from Mary Orphan as if a mild wind turned their faces in another direction. They moved without looking back.

Mary Orphan stood there motionless. Eventually, after even I felt uncomfortable because she was just standing there, she dropped her shoulders and looked down. She tucked her right foot right up to her buttocks in the ballerina stance, then with a sudden swing like a football player, she kicked something on the ground. She turned around, and we looked at one another. Her eyes were consuming everything ahead of her. She then dropped her head again.

'It's a good thing it was not a rock you kicked at,' I tried.

'It's a good thing it was not your chin.' She smiled.

She had the gentlest eyes ever when her mood was good. I always felt as if she understood. When her brown eyes looked into the blue sky, it seemed to have a calming effected on her.

'Can you hear that?' I probed, pointing to the heavens.

'No, what?' She looked around. 'Come on, what are you hearing?'

'Listen. Come on, listen. Pancakes calling . . . pancakes calling,' I sang.

'You would like that. You like eating pancakes.' She placed her hands on her hips and said, 'So, what's new?'

'Will you join me?' I invited.

'Only if I may have two, please,' she bargained.

We queued at the pancake stall. She told me what was bothering her. 'They can be nice to me in school, but if they group up, everyone is nasty to me, because I'm an orphan—and I'm also not an orphan, you see. That's why.' She cried, and I hugged her.

Then one of the teachers saw me. I had not heard her among the crowd. She lifted me up by the ear. My left foot was a few centimetres from the ground. As she dropped me to the ground she said, 'You must concentrate on your schoolwork and leave the girl alone.'

Mary Orphan tried to defend me. 'Mrs May, he did not mean to be nasty—'

'And as for you, young lady,' she shouted on, 'you should take an example from the other girls over there.' She pointed to the 'saints' who had just rejected Mary Orphan in such a 'holy' manner. 'I will get you expelled from this school,' Mrs May threatened. 'Even if I don't, I will make your life miserable until you leave.' Then she left the scene in a huff.

Eventually we got to the front of the queue. We ordered eight pancakes. One of the mothers served us, and I noticed she added two extra pancakes to the packet. 'We just asked for eight, Mrs Rose,' I reminded her.

She smiled. 'That's okay. It's on the house.'

'I will pay for it,' I said. 'I do have money.' I did not welcome charity, and I did not want us to feel like 'orphans'. Then Mary Orphan kicked my ankle, and with her head tilted to an angle, she said, 'Take it. Take it.' And another kick followed.

Mrs Rose noticed my discomfort. 'See it as a discount,' she suggested. 'I've given you a discount.'

'Thank you, Mrs Rose,' Mary said as she jumped in front of me. 'We appreciate it.' And she dragged me along.

'She talks like the Indians on the other side of Hannover Avenue,' I concluded.

'Yes, my dad says they don't have fixed jobs like at the railways and post office, but they always have money, because they know how to wheel and deal.' Mary Orphan raised her eyebrows and offered me a pancake.

'I have to see a doctor on Monday,' I told her. 'I am sort of scared.'

'Why?' she asked with pancake stuffed in her mouth. 'Why?' again she asked after swallowing. 'That's what they did to me,' she said. 'Then my mom and dad went to court. I told you, you know.'

'My parents say they will first see if I have enough brains after the test with the doctor.'

'What do you mean?' she asked, sounding confused.

'I told them I want to go to a boarding school. My mother said *no!* And my father said it may be a good idea, but the test will prove if I have brains to go or not.'

Mary Orphan then became very sad; she turned her back on me and walked a few meters ahead. Then she turned to me again. 'You are a real friend to me, but if you have to go, will you please write and visit me during the holidays?' She seemed to be panicked.

We enjoyed that day with all its drama.

'Oh no, there is my mother,' she said. 'I will need to take her home before she embarrasses me. See you Monday,' she said, giving me a friendly punch on my shoulder.

Monday morning I arrived early at school. I placed my schoolbag on the usual spot and stood at a pillar wondering what was awaiting me. She crept up from behind and covered my eyes with her hands. She did not even whisper.

'Do I have three guesses?' She still kept silent. 'Do I have four guesses? So you don't want me to guess?' Still she upheld her silence. 'Then I will make one guess only and . . . tickle you!' and Mary got away just in time.

'When and how will you go to the doctor?' she asked.

'Good morning to you two,' said Mr Ronaldson, our maths teacher, from behind us. 'He will be going by bus.' Then he turned to me. 'Don't be too worried about it. You should do just fine.'

I was happy for his vote of confidence in me.

'And yes, Mary, he will be okay,' Mr Ronaldson assured.

Off I went on that bus, by myself, on my way to that unknown destiny.

I walked into a huge building. The office was enormous. It was very quiet . . . almost scary. Then the silence was interrupted. 'Are you here to see Dr Johnson?' the secretary asked.

'What type of a doctor is he?' I inquired.

'Don't worry, he is not the type that gives injections,' she assured.

'I am not afraid of injections,' I replied, trying to be brave.

'Okay, here is his office, and you are welcome to ask him yourself,' she said with a smile.

The doctor looked 'okay' to talk with; he did not seem like one who would bite off your head.

'What's on your mind?' he asked

'Why am I here? Am I also going to an orphanage? I would rather go to a boarding school. What must I do here?' My questions were many.

Dr Johnson made a gesture with his hand that invited me in. 'Please be seated. Your principal requested you do a test to determine how they best could help you,' he explained. 'But first tell me why you would prefer to be in a boarding school.' It was a serious question.

'It's difficult to study at home, and I sleep in the lounge. My brother and sisters cry at night when Mom and Dad argue . . . or . . .' It was difficult to answer the doctor.

This doctor maintained a friendly but 'strait' face. For a split second, he dropped his eyes; at the same time, his throat indicated a nervous swallowing. He looked up at me again with eyes that seemed wondering. 'Let's do the tests, okay?' he said. 'We will do them over a few days.'

'Okay!'

'Then we will be clear on the whole matter. Shall we start?'

I agreed. For some reason it felt as if this was the most important test of my life. When I got home, I would not answer my mother's questions for fear that she would hold me back from going to boarding school.

The long days at the doctor's office finally ended. The doctor made me feel human, worthy of a good future. 'Now go out there and conquer the world,' he said, shaking my hand.

It was good to be back at school again. That afternoon the intercom interrupted maths. 'Mr Ronaldson, I have time to see the two of you now,' the principal ordered.

Mr Ronaldson took me along. We walked past the classroom where Mary Orphan was. She knew what it was all about, and I knew she was stressed.

The distance to the headmasters' office was not far; however, it felt as if the journey lasted forever.

Again, you are welcome just for a few moments to join me in the long walk to judgment. 'Green Mile experience? Electric chair? Verbal torture? Expulsion? Orphanage?

We slowed down at the door marked 'Principal', and Mr Ronaldson knocked on the door. The answering 'Come in' sounded certain, like an order given at cadet parade. Then we stepped into a large office.

He sat on the other side of a big table, looked at me over his reading glasses, then took off the glasses and put them down. 'Tell me, young man, what do you want to become one day? What type of work do you see yourself doing?'

Startled, I searched for words. 'I could have my own shop. I could be a minister of religion. I think I would make a good detective, or even a doctor. But I need to go to boarding school. Can I go to boarding school . . . please?'

'I can only recommend that for you, but you'll need your parents' consent.' He stood up, picked up a brown envelope, and walked around the table. 'Do you know what is in this?' He seemed to become quite exited. He turned to the teacher. 'Mr Ronaldson, this young boy's report states that he is more than capable . . . ,' Then threw the envelope on the floor and jumped on it. Yes, he jumped on it. '*You*,' he said, 'can go to the best universities in the world . . . Cambridge . . . Harvard . . . and . . .' He looked at me, seemingly exasperated. 'This is the most frustrating thing to see,' he said. 'Other children's parents charm teachers for special attention for their children, and they even do their children's homework! You can!' and looked me in the eye. 'Just do your best for yourself.'

Mr Ronaldson looked surprised, yet relieved. But the headmaster wasn't finished. 'Now, Mr Ronaldson, I need you to convey this to his other teachers. Please let us help to get the best out of this youngster. Let's understand his living situation. Will you do that for us?' In an empathetic, assertive manner, the headmaster closed the discussion.

I was quite relieved, but wondered if I would have my parents' consent. On our way back to the classroom, I wondered what the best way would be to approach my parents.

I then saw Mary Orphan outside her classroom, head hanging, shoulders dropped and playing with her fingernails. Her teacher had made her stand outside for lack of concentration.

Realizing we were close to her, she stood up straight. She turned in our direction, arms straight and open hands facing us, eyes wide open and lips tight on one another, with that 'must I wait longer to find out what's up' look.

'I am going to be fine, and they're not sending me away.' It was the statement she desperately needed to hear. The life-giving power made her face light up again.

'Okay, I believe it's time for you to get back into your classroom, Mary,' said Mr Ronaldson, opening the door. 'Mrs May,' he said to Mary's teacher, 'Mary will be just fine.'

It was good for Mary Orphan's best friend to know that he had enough brains.

Whatever! It did not get me the boarding school consent.

Does social kindness not show the recognition of human worthiness?—Wynie

8

Papa . . . protect my daughter . . . safe money

In the winter months that August, I turned fifteen. The winds brought me a wonderful yet a shocking and mind-blowing surprise. A friend's sister was standing in the passage with a small, wrapped-up something that looked like a box. However, her smile was soft, yet wondering, and she managed to let the words out: 'I . . . we . . . I got you a present. Happy birthday!' Then she kissed me. Wow! I had kissed a few times before, but not with willing lips like hers!

It was so good. I felt her lips and tasted the real thing. Those soft eyes were looking at me tenderly. Her eyelids lifted just to open and give me a better view of her green, sparkling eyes.

'We kissed . . . we kissed,' she said softly. Slowly she let her chin down and looked at me from under her eyelids, blushing!

I stepped forward and hugged her. Then, my sister, at the top of her voice shouted, 'Mommy! Mommy, Anita gave Alwyn a . . . a . . . present.' Thank goodness she did not say 'kiss', for I would have never had peace or freedom ever after.

My introduction to what a kiss should be like was great, and I carried that thought with me for quite some time. I am sure Anita's father noticed the sparkle from our eyes.

You see he had warned her that my intentions were physical and had nothing to do with being attracted to her. Anita's mom went ballistic; for the first time she had to deal with her daughter's feelings, and you can be sure Anita knew what she wanted.

'My daughter will not have just a middle-class life! She will one day meet a good boy from a wealthy family.' She made sure her voice carried the message to the neighbours'' windows. 'And Papa . . . it's your responsibility to protect my daughter.'

Eventually her father had to talk to me in a 'convincing manner', and I broke it up. Then, her heart was so sore, but she now understood why her father forbade me from visiting there again.

Therefore, I had to look like the bad boy. I still wonder, if she had to know the truth, how Anita would have viewed her daddy.

Her mom and dad had a vision of their daughter as educated and secure with a 'husband of high social standing.' Anita now turned into a rebel. 'Okay, Mommy and Daddy, I'll do just that.' And sarcasm thrived.

After a few months, Anita found such a hunk, born and raised by parents of 'high social standing'. He was called Victor; her mom referred to him as Vic when she bragged about her daughter's boyfriend's father's business. 'He comes from the north, you know,' was her famous 'bragging rights' statement. In those days, the north of Johannesburg was a wealthy area.

In the meantime, the next owner of the shop where I worked had been introduced to me. I had seen a few owners come and go. Now Jose had a vision for his shop, serving mainly the factory workers on weekdays and soccer match crowds over the weekends. Spectators and players flooded the fridge doors that stored the drinks they needed to rinse their thirst away.

Jose loved the night and weekend life, and spoiled the woman that dared to spoil him. 'Alwyn,' he would say, 'I can trust you . . . I am taking my girl away for a long dirty weekend. I want you to open and close my shop . . . and only you and the assistant work, okay?'

The weekend was a busy one. On Saturday and Sunday league soccer was the order of the day, and rush hour had no equal—smokes, Coke, chocolate, and buns stuffed with cheese, cold meats, and patties topped with fries. Hotdogs, fish and chips, Coke and Coke and Coke—that 'black holy water' . . . the 'drug of life' for all who needed to wash down their food.

On Sunday afternoon, she walked in. I had not seen her in a long time. She had disappeared around the middle of December—birthday

33

time—and was nowhere to be found. She turned from the fridge with cool drink in hand. Our eyes met with surprise. 'You still work here all this time?'

'Hi, yes . . . how is it going in school these days?' I asked for the sake of her new boyfriend.

'School's good. Mom drops me at the bus stop every morning, and Dad picks us up every evening at Mom's work.' She put her money on the counter. I opened the till and took out the change. 'How are you doing . . . with your rugby?' she asked.

'No matches this weekend,' I said, placing the change in Anita's hand. 'Easter is an off weekend.'

'Anita—doll—you done?' Hunk hung onto her neck, extending a greeting hand and with a singing, dance-swinging voice. 'I am Vickie,' he informed me. 'And my school days are long gone. I'm leaving it to you youngsters, pal.' And he dragged Anita out.

As they were walking out the door he turned to her and spoke. I heard a bit of what he had to say: 'This loser . . . working in the shop, where did you . . .' And his voice faded as the distance increased.

The next afternoon, Anita's mother walked in to buy a few things. 'Good afternoon, Mrs Meyer.'

'Good afternoon. Vogue please . . . you know my brand.'

'Will that be all, Mrs Meyer?'

'One white . . . and one brown bread, please.'

'On its way.' And I noticed that this woman seemed to be beside herself, but was controlling her mood with effort.

'And . . . and milk. And you can prepare two pieces of fish for the hubby and me.' Her mind seemed to be all over the place, only occasionally returning to where she was.

'Did you enjoy your long weekend, Mrs Meyer?' I dared.

In an upright position and with friendly mask, she said 'Of course, we always do . . .' Then she hesitated.

I had noticed that her dress and make-up were in a neglected state, and this wasn't the first time I had noticed her thus.

'How is Anita doing in the new school?' I asked. 'She has always done so well.'

'We will have to wait and see . . . she's been bunking school . . . or bonking the boyfriend.' I noticed a mother's disproval.

'Bonking?' I questioned.

'Naive, you are . . . better so for you . . . and a girl, should you have one.' There were tears just under her eyelids.

Mrs Meyer had everything on her list, and the till revealed the sum total. She paid, and a silence hung in the air. She turned away and walked off. At the door, she turned back. 'If you do not want to break your mother and father's hearts . . .' She swallowed a few times, then said, 'Don't use drugs . . .' Then she turned her head and speedily walked away.

She was a broken mother. Her expectations for high success and social status for her daughter had been shattered, so even had been her heart.

It was time for cashing up after the day's takings. I closed the shop door and went through the everyday ritual. It took a while, then I placed the moneybag and envelope on the top shelf, just as Jose had instructed. I locked the safe and locked the shop. The long weekend was finally over, and I was going home to get some rest. When my head hit my pillow, however, I struggled to fall asleep. Anita's mom's words kept echoing thought my mind: 'My daughter will not have just a middle-class life! She will one day meet a good boy from a wealthy family. And Papa . . . it's your responsibility to protect my daughter.' I was wondering about my own three sisters and brother . . . and finally I fell asleep.

'Alwyn, wake up . . . wake up,' my mother called. 'Jose tells me the money in the safe is missing!'

Mom and Dad looked at me as if they were thinking, 'Is our son a thief? No, he's not. What do we believe?' I was quickly out of sleep mode.

'I put the money in the safe, and then I locked it. Here's the safe key,' I explained as I walked down the passage to the front door.

Mom was shocked. 'Yes, Jose said the safe was locked, but there is a big amount missing.'

'He is the only other person with a key,' I said, 'so he can blame me . . . and that is not fair.' I was now sorry for agreeing to look after the shop and assuming all the responsibility that went with the task.

Jose was drunk; I could smell him from a distance. 'On my mother's life, the money is gone,' he moaned. 'I trusted you with all I have. How

35

can you do that after I trusted you? The previous owner said you could be trusted. Now you . . . my safe is empty . . . on our lady . . . my money is gone,' he cried.

Startled by all of this, my mother was upset. 'Come,' I said, 'let's go to the shop and see if we can understand what happened.' We marched to the store.

'It's no good. The money is gone . . . but you will see.' Jose was still crying. 'Alwyn, how could you do this to me . . . how could you?'

We got to the shop. Jose had closed the door, but had not locked it. We went in and went directly to the safe, which was now unlocked. Jose opened the safe door. 'See, it is gone! My money is gone!'

'But there is the money bag and envelope. I put in the money from the whole of the weekend,' I pointed out.

'I had a bag here full of notes . . . a lot of money . . . now it gone . . . I trusted you,' said the crying Jose.

'Where was it?' I got irritated, and only then did I realized he was referring to other money that I was not aware of.

'Down there . . . at the bottom. There was a plastic bag with money rolled in it. Thousands of rand . . . I trusted you,' he said in his drunken woe.

I bent down and realized there was a drawer. I opened it and found the plastic bag full of cash. 'What the f&^% is this?' I demanded. I was angry.

Skinny Jose's eye became larger than his ears. His mouth opened as he placed his hands on his head. 'That is my money! Oh thank God,' he said with a hysterical cry. 'You see, I *can* trust you . . . I love you, Alwyn, I love you . . .'

Jose did not get what he expected, did he? And so it had been with his dirty weekend as well. She had taken him for a ride and had gone after his money . . . sucked him dry.

Must the mind be shocked by controversy to awaken in life? —*Wynie*

9

Banned for life the day I started

When I was between the ages of fifteen and sixteen, I experienced one of those experimental times, and I felt up to the challenge of all that went on in life. I was fed up with all the other boys' 'I am' attitudes. They gathered in groups manipulating and influencing one another into hypnotic states.

On an emotional high, with cigarettes in hand, the group members found power in numbers, and things went out of control. Everyone who was not sucking and blowing smoke, or puffing and living up to the task was a 'jerk' or a 'loser' of some type. They asserted that those who had no smoking aspirations had a shortfall with little less than a peanut-sized brain. Those who smoked belong to a special elite group, chosen by a divine power and blessed with special gifts that might quite possibly liberate the human race.

They were leaning over the walls with cigarettes pinched between two fingers, suggesting a V sign. With the filter hanging from their lips they would roll their eyes as they drew air into the burning end. They would find great pleasure as the smoke flowed through the tobacco in the paper tube, through the filter, and into their lungs.

Then with some mystical wonder, their mouths would transform into the shape of old coffee kettles and 'trumpet' as smoke rushed out like steam from a train in some Western movie, waiting patiently for passengers to get onboard. Only those boys who were cigarette wise, who showed that they could, were welcome to ride.

They were not going to make me smoke. Oh no, bud. No one was going to 'twist my arm' without my consent; it was part of my life's motto, and I had learned to live by it. However, when I was this young age, schooling from 'life's tutor' had many lessons up its sleeve.

It seemed that all of humanity were smokers. They were all over. Coke, cigarettes, bread, and milk seemed to be on the shopping list of every customer who came into the store. Dad, at times, would say, 'Ten thousand mine workers smoke Lexington.' And that bore evidence of 'after action satisfaction'—the motto of the brand.

One cloudy afternoon, I hit the road in the direction of the primary school, a distance from home. I went at about four in the afternoon, as the factory workers were on their daily, run-of-the-mill walk to the railway station. I found my spot behind the big pine trees standing tall. If I'd wanted to put my arms around one if them, there would have had to be three of me. At the southwest corner of the school, just outside its fence, they stood like skyscrapers. The top branches, with windscreen wiper motion, wiped the dust from the sky. The factory workers knew me from the shop, and day in and day out they passed the corner where our house stood.

The rain was sure to fall, and a man had to do what he had to do. I took one cigarette out of the pack of ten and made it hang from my lips; it made me feel as tall as the trees, standing my ground. After placing the pack back into my pocket, I pulled out the matchbox so I could start this divine ritual that would empower me for self-esteem, confidence, and for membership in the districts of the elite. This would enable me to act out that 'I am the man' stance . . . to suggest that 'I belong', 'I am brave, willing, and capable'.

The rain was falling—a drop here and a drop there, at a rhythm that slowly increased. Some of those on their way to the railway station had umbrellas, while some had cardboard boxes in various shapes covering themselves from the approaching storm. Some were running and just looked at me and shook their heads. One Zulu man shouted, 'Now you think you're a man.'

'Buzz off. Your train will not wait!' I shouted as I covered the lit match with my hands protecting it from the wind.

Another said, 'I am going to tell your mother.' The statement pierced my ears.

I dropped the match as yet another crossed the road, approaching the 'man' about to become the 'I am' of town.

Now two of them, with concerned facial expressions, said what was on their mind, thereby showing emotions that needed to surface. '*Hau*! You do not need to smoke. We know you well, from the shop, and we know your mother. You are not like the other young ones. Don't waste your life.' This concluded their 'speech'.

'*Hau*, just leave me,' I responded. 'Why do black people worry about a white boy?' I was trying to put them off. 'Your train is waiting.'

'The trains are many. We get home late anyway, and a few minutes later isn't a problem,' one reasoned.

'Your smoking is a problem,' the other added. 'We like the 'white' boy.

'It's my choice, so leave me,' I said, waving my hands.

'Yes, children's choices are stupid. Are you stupid?' They finally left, much to my relief.

The transformation was going to be activated when I did the real thing. I was going to renew myself, to replace the boy with the man, finally. The cigarette was hanging from my lips. The match and box connected to ignite a magical flame that would cause the start of a revolution, if two parents were to find out. Yet among this generation, I would be part of the teenage evolution.

A small flame at the end of a match was just surviving the wind's attack. Following the wind was a fine shower that had the effect of a forceful sprinkler. It wiped my dusty face with an invisible cloth. Like the animals of the fields turning their back to the wind and rain, I turned to protect this sacred event of reincarnation from the elements of nature.

The small fire started giving life to the most divine smell coming from this cylindrical tobacco structure. Puffing did the job. 'I am smoking . . . I am smoking.' Reason filled my mind. The feeling was good, yet another suggestion entered my mind: 'Don't puff! Smoke like a man.' A statement made to many an aspiring smoker.

For this 'man' would not wait upon himself to prove such stature; he would follow the word of those who spoke 'wisdom' unto the daring young 'men' of the future.

Action followed the thought of a creative mind, recalling that a 'man' pulls the smoke into his lungs to fullness, then a 'man' holds it there for just a few seconds until he experiences the floating-high feeling. Then, by a slow steady exhale, a man releases all the stress and experiences freedom that the 'man' will need from time to time. 'After-action satisfaction . . .'

My mind was light years ahead of this activity. The act of holding in the smoke got it all stuck somewhere between the bowels and nose, and none of the orifices was willing to cooperate.

Then, by some wonder, nature intervened by its own unique surprise: the air pipes were forced open with the output of a fireball cannon as the lighting struck from the heavens and found its way though the pine tree branches, no more than a meter ahead of this distressed 'man'.

Through coughing, tears, and the shivers, this 'man' noticed the evidence of a heavenly 'whip' engraved on the tar road.

Pedestrians witnessed heaven's lashes, and they surrounded me at a distance. You could call us all pale-faces, as we all had shocked expressions on our faces. It was quiet for a while until shock had one of the women in tears. '*Hau! Hau!* You can die when that lightning hits you!'

Another said, 'You see, God has spoken: *no smoking* for you!'

'Hey, white boy, trying to be clever? Are you mad?' Came the voice from the back of the group. Pointing in my direction, he continued, 'Come, give us the smokes. You can't use it.'

Out came the 'pack of ten'. I handed it over.

'Hey "whitey", first time and you use Ritmeester cigars! *Hau* the Big Master was saying *no!* Okay?'

'Ha! Go home now and have sugar water,' a woman cried out.

Yet another teasing, 'I am going to tell your mother now.'

Back home, Mother looked at me with that 'what happened to you' frown on her face.

'I think I am sick,' was all I could say. She believed that one.

The 'chosen smoking brethren' gathered around their holy match-striking ceremony once again, bowing their heads to the holy fire protected in the hollows of their hands, bringing cigarettes and fire into the sacrificial altar, exchanging fresh air with contamination that would smoke out all stress, fear, and inferiority complexes. 'You want to join us, brother?' The question sounded like a welcoming invitation to be part of the chosen group.

The neighbours' son offered a Camel. 'Break his back and join the caravan, bro.'

'Th—thank you . . . ,' came over these lips. I did not believe what I'd just said. 'I mean *no* thank you.' My mind filled with the previous day's drama as I wondered about how I would be the rejected one.

They jeered and then their "cheerleader" sang their praises: 'Jerk!' 'Loser!' F*@&-off!'

I had to stand tall as those trees. 'The day I started was the day I stopped.' It just came out.

'Bro, what are you tuning? What did you sniff today?' Cheerleader sang again.

'I had one Strike and stopped. After thousands of "match strikes", you will find it hard to stop.'

Cheerleader sang to those around him passionately. Swinging his hands and gesturing with his fingers and fists, he transformed into a conducting lunatic. He wasn't directing a symphony of musical instruments though.

I became the outcast. Therefore, in the 'holy union', I was banned for life.

Does effect not follow cause with unvarying certainty? —Wynie

10

Mother's running shoes

Michelle and Steven were not twins, but everyone was convinced that they were. They had one mother and two fathers. No, do not go there. Let me explain.

Michelle's mother did not know that she was pregnant with her firstborn when she received the sad news that her child's father had been in a fatal accident.

Michelle's mother, Alison, had been a top athlete in her high school and college days. She was attractive and got the attention of everyone; all looked at Alison as the next great international athlete. Her beauty had many a man mesmerized, until her 'lock, stock and smoking barrel' moment arrived that summer's day when she was jogging to warm up before a big event.

'Douglas, a hundred-meter sprinter just passed by, and he caught my eye,' Alison used to say. 'Douglas's voice commanded my ears, his look and smile had me spellbound. And he was tall . . . handsome.' She spoke as if she was in the moment again. 'With my feet unstable, my mind and heart occupied and jumping summersaults, I ran off and lost a place in that important race.' Alison had yet another goal in mind; his name—Douglas.

Mrs Alison Nell, with her baby Michelle in a pram, was roaming the aisles of a major supermarket. She turned from one aisles in to the other and collided with a hunk of a man. She looked to see if her eyes were conveying the actual picture. Standing tall in front of her was Raymond, her first love. They were both so happy to have met by accident, and they embraced one another. The result? Steven. Steven was a bigger boy and looked just like his older sister, which is why so many people thought they were twins.

Michelle's school career was also highlighted with academics as well as athletics. She went from one podium to another.

I was two years younger than Michelle. Discovering that Michelle did not have many friends, I asked her what would make her the happiest girl in the world and why. 'You ask these questions that nobody asks, but I don't mind telling you.' And, in a hesitant, soft but clear voice, she said, 'To live in a boarding school, nowhere near my mom.'

'Nowhere near your mom?' I was shocked and surprised. 'It is like I am hearing myself!'

'Yes, you heard me. I love my mom but . . .'

Her mom walked in, 'Thanks dear . . . but what?'

'Oh, Mom, must you always be so inquisitive? Pay more attention to what your husband is doing. He adores you but—and here is where the big "but" comes in—you love only yourself.'

'You're . . . a little *bitch!* How dare you talk to me in this way? How dare you!' she cried out. 'I will get to you later.'

Alison walked down the passage. When she entered the dining room, she stopped and caressed her old spiked running shoes: a trophy awarded to Alison, by Alison, with compliments from Alison.

Alison looked at us and, with an ominous grin on her face, said, 'You youngsters must put your minds on being something one day. And you, Michelle, must pay more attention to your sport if you want to be on the international stage.' Her voice was bewitching. Then she walked out of the front door, slamming it behind her as she left for tea with an important associate.

'And she called *me* a bitch,' said Michelle with tears in her eyes. 'Does that answer your entire question—friend?'

The end of the year arrived very quickly. Michelle's schooling was brilliant, and she earned a college bursary. She also received an invitation to join a South African athletic group that would provide her with a chance to represent the country internationally.

In the middle of December, Michelle's brother, Steven, invited me over as usual. We were in training: skipping rope, shadow boxing, and working with the punching bag that hung in the garage. Then, just as we were putting on the gloves, I heard those familiar words: 'You little *bitch!*'

Steven's father came through the door onto the patio, and his mother, spewing language that did not belong to this planet, followed behind him. 'You are a father's backside! Talk sense into Michelle's head!' She spat her words with fury.

'Yes, Dad did.' Michelle made her appearance. 'He always does. It's not something you did too often, Mother.'

Then, from behind her back, Michelle took out her mother's 'trophy' running shoes and held them up. 'These are yours, Mother. They do not fit me. They never will. You see, I never wanted to be like you. And hear me now once and for all.' She put the trophy on the patio table.

Her mother held her chest as if she had to keep it in place. 'But, sweetheart . . .' she began with the voice of the archangel himself.

'I am not running your race anymore,' stated Michelle. 'And as of February I will not be living here anymore.' She walked away.

Alison transformed into a statue; her soul found it impossible to move.

Why will one live in the shadow of another, and not preserve individuality?
—*Wynie*

11

They surprise you . . . they shock you

I always found it interesting to observe older people—adults. In a ladies' bar, in a corner close to the door, I sat with paper and pen in hand jotting down all I heard and saw.

I have never been disappointed by my fellow man, for they always provide me with shocking surprises.

'You bitch! You flirted with that man,' one man said to his crying girlfriend. 'Next time you do that, I'll kill you.' He went on and on.

I picked up my glass to sip my Rock shanty when Mr Muscle Man came up to me, pierced my skull with his eyes, and moved his lips. 'You like to do something about it, pal?'

I anticipated executing a left jab to his chin, a right hook to meet up with the short rib, and a cross with my left to meet the side of his jaw. I was ready.

His girlfriend's statement, however, knocked me out. 'Gordon, may I remind you that it was only a few days ago that I had to pull someone off you. Stop your shit,' she commanded.

She turned to me. 'Aren't you too young to be in this joint?'

'I'm—I—I'm studying human nature,' was my quick though shaky response. I pointed out my pen and paper.

She grabbed the notes out of my hand and had a quick glance at them. Then she called to Gordon and made him sit down and listen as she read aloud:

When I open these eyes, every day, it's about people.
Whether they're inside or outside—they're there.

You see them . . . hear every word they say. More than one
message people convey.

Some are happy, some are not. Everyone else seems fine
until an unhappy mood surfaces from the heart.

Wherever I go and whatever I hear, no matter how and
why, by their anger, tears, joy, or fears, the most important
thing I hear . . . relationships.

He said this. He said that. I will not tolerate it . . . How
dare he talk to me like that?

Adults don't impress me at all—for they have a shortfall.

They want to be happy, yet they fight. They need love,
yet they hate. They want to be trusted, however they do not
trust others.

And those I thought were happy and true kept up the act
only for a while.

Now, I see their bulls^#* . . . from a mile.

Gordon looked at me and asked my name. Then he said, 'How old are you?'

'I'm sixteen today, and you, sir?'

'Thirty-five.' We looked one another in the eye.

The movement of his irises had me wondering what he was thinking and feeling. Then at one stage, his eyes turned soft. He looked so cool. The corners of his eyes closed as a smile appeared on his face. 'You cannot make me feel bad,' he said. Then he stood up and said, 'Be careful you don't become a "ladies' man" some day.' Then he made me leave.

I walked across the road to my next destination, the movies. The queue was long. *A good movie must be showing*, I thought. My attention was gripped by a couple kissing, and someone was complaining about the ticket sales being slow.

A mother appeared from nowhere; her voice echoed to every ear. 'My son is only seventeen, you slut! You are twenty-something! What are you teaching my son?'

My eyes and ears were on alert, for real life was entertaining me.

A few places in front of me, a man of about fifty stepped out of the queue and got himself a cool drink. On returning to his place, the woman behind him shared a piece of her mind: 'I did not keep your place for you. You did not even ask! Why do you just assume that you can do that?' She sniped away at the tall man.

His face flushed as his eyes grew bigger. His jaw pulled his mouth open, and his tongue gave evidence of what he had been drinking.

She went on: 'I hope for your sake your wife can live with that sort of behaviour.'

'You're right,' the tall man said with confidence. 'My wife would not have given that insulting mouth of yours a backhand; rather, she would have shared a list of all my good qualities.'

The red haired, green-eyed woman, dressed in a white mini, took a step backwards.

The man continued. 'I would have loved to introduce her to you, but it's been about six months since she passed away. For now, I will put my mother on to you. However I'll have to get the old age home to bring her to your place.' His eyes had that daring look about them. 'Please let me have your details to arrange the meeting,' he finished.

Her face turned red in such a way that her freckles went into hiding.

There was yet another couple standing in the shade of the building, or rather should I say hanging onto one another for dear life in a close embrace. The wall of the building seemed to be part of the miracle, as it kept them sort of in a standing position.

A soft 'dong' indicated that the movie was about to start. The last few people walked in, and the door closed. You could hear the reels turn before sound filled the cinema. The picture appeared on the screen, and all eyes fixed on the coming attractions. The mood had changed by now. After a while, the intermission provided a few minutes for a smoke break.

Entering the gents, I heard this discussion. 'Oh, man, I don't need your protection.' This was said in a deep voice.

'Yes you do, pal. I'm your guardian angel, and you will pay protection money. If you don't, you will have to pay someone to protect you from me!' The second voice responded in a cold, cruel manner.

I heard the toilet flush, and at the same time I heard a grunting and growling. I quickly started to wash my hands before the toilet door opened. I expected two people to come from behind the door, but only one appeared. He must have seen the amazement on my face. 'How long have you been standing here?' he asked.

'I just walked in,' I said and continued washing my hands.

'And you are washing hands? Bull s#i&!' Then he made his flick knife visible. 'This area is full of danger, *brother*,' he threatened. 'Hope you can take care of yourself.' His whole persona made him look like a member of the mafia, as they are represented in the movies.

Back in the lobby, relieved to be away from all the toilet incidents, I turned my full attention on everyone around me. 'Freckled Redhead Lady' and 'Tall Chap' were on good speaking terms by now, and . . . she was giggling. *Wonder why?*

The other two were still hanging onto one another; they could not get closer, believe me, unless they went home. A soft and friendly woman's words attempted to disconnect them: 'It is interval, sweethearts, so take a break.' And we all stepped in for the main movie.

Laurel and Hardy's *Nothing But Trouble* filled the screen. As viewers watched, some laughed; others had tears in their eyes. I studied every person in that cinema. I saw dozens of different emotions on people's faces in the space of a short time—joy, anticipation, surprise, shock, shame, wonder, and many more.

The 'Lip-Sucking Sweethearts' now took the earlier advice to the limit; their suction systems were at rest as they fixed their eyes upon that screen.

'Mommy's Little Boy' and twenty-something 'Spider Lady'? Well now, Hollywood could have had a record profit on that scene. With octopus-like movement, Spider Lady and her man tangled in action. Their hands were all over—first his then hers. His hands disappeared into her 'comfort zone' as he cupped a size C. She chewed his fingers and snacked on his ears.

Spider Lady made his head disappear into her comfort zone. He looked like mommy's boy, however, in the arms of a bolder woman who did not pass on essential nutrition to vital developing organs.

Two rows in front of them to their right, next to the wall, a young lady's face showed that she was evidently not amazed by what was on screen; instead, with her hand over her mouth, she was obviously casting her attention to Spider Lady's ecstatic gaze.

I threw popcorn, and when it landed on Spider Lady, she grabbed a jacket to cover her occupied bosom. By that time, I had my only imagination to entertain me on how Mommy's Little Boy indulged himself among the hills of her 'comfort zone'.

A few minutes later, the brightness of the cinema lights indicated that the movie had come to an end.

Being one of the last to leave the cinema—for obvious reasons—I exited the building, turned right on the walkway, and turned my attention to yet another gathering of human beings.

In front of the fire department building, a person was lying face down. Many people gathered around. Redhead Freckled Lady was on her knees, acting as paramedic. Bloodstains were on the shirt of the man on the ground. 'Done with a knife,' one said as I pushed through the crowd.

Guardian Angel turned around, and I saw agonizing and intense pain revealed on his face. His eyes were looking at the floor, as if he was in a trance, hoping that he was wakening from a dream. His flick knife was still intact.

He picked up his head and saw me. 'Go away! *Just go away!*'

'I—hope you'll be . . .' He looked at the medic not wanting to hear from me.

'*Just go away!*' Again he screamed at the top of his voice.

The police officer asked, 'Did this youngster attack you?'

'No! Just let him go.'

'No!' an older woman confirmed. 'I was a witness to the incident. Two men jumped from a car and attacked him with short knives.' She had the police officer's attention.

Tall Chap and his Redhead Freckled Lady companion walked me home.

'What a day! Life is real, Dad,' I told my father. 'You see people in many situations. They surprise you . . . shock you. People pretend to be what they are not. Why, Dad? Why would a man speak to his woman in public like that—"Next time you do that, I'll kill you"? Why, Dad?'

49

Dad stood up, walked closer, and looked at me. 'Watch and learn, my boy. Watch and learn. And don't "why, Dad" me.'

End of discussion.

'Where did we get this child?' he asked, turning to my mom.

'Ha-ha, it was cross insemination,' she replied sarcastically.

Should one fall on battleground, or will one rise on fertile ground? —Wynie

12

Boy from the North . . . boy from the South

From time to time, I used the bus service to explore other suburbs of Johannesburg. I was quite familiar with areas in the west and east, but now I had the northern suburbs and its people in my sight—places like Greenside and Rosebank.

The bus stopped, and I got off. It was new territory. 'Where am I?' I thought aloud. I noticed a street sign that told me I was on Jan Smuts Avenue. There were many more luxury cars on the streets than I was used to seeing where I came from, and many people, especially women, were walking walk out of shops carrying more and bigger parcels than shoppers I was used to watching. I knew I would have to check it out.

When I walked into a pharmacy, my X-ray eyes covered every corner and every surface possible. It was different here; not all the goods were stacked on top of one another. There were expensive goods I never saw in pharmacies I was used to. I was admiring it all, but then I heard: 'Watch that boy. He is not from here.'

I looked around to see where that boy might be. Seeing no other boy, I realized that the man must have been talking about me. 'Sir, I am just looking around . . .'

'Good! Only looking . . . not pocketing,' the older man behind the counter warned with a piercing stare and cold eyes that penetrated my soul.

The assistant—the front shop lady—then made her voice heard as she spoke to a customer. 'Mrs Gins, we just received new perfumes all the way from Paris. It would be a sin to let this opportunity pass you by.'

'Why did you not mention that earlier? Do I have to draw everything out of you?' Mrs Gins replied, chin up and ready to place her hand in her handbag. As soon as she'd heard 'all the way from Paris', you know, out came her chequebook.

'That's lovely,' said the wealthy customer, sniffing the perfume proffered by the assistant. 'At tennis on Wednesday the girls will smell me coming from a mile away.'

'That will be two hundred and twenty rand, Mrs Gins.' I watched as the cash register completed its calculation.

I stood closer as Mrs Gins started writing the cheque. *Wow that's about what Dad earns per week*, I thought. I wondered what work she did. *And today is Wednesday, and she's not working—like a doctor.*

I walked out of the pharmacy, shocked. *That lady did not ask what it cost. She just paid. She must have a large budget.* It took me a while to digest what I had just seen.

A few meters ahead on the sidewalk, two women were sitting at a table in serious discussion. 'You don't say. Are you serious?' the older one ask.

When I was only a meter or two away, I decided to have a drink. *I need to hear how these two ladies resolve their problem.* My old habit prevailed again. I sat not too far from them with my good ear turned in their direction. I made sure I also had a reasonable view.

'Yes, and he pushed me so hard that I fell and bumped my head!' the victim complained.

'Haven't you had enough of him my, dear? Divorce the bas . . .' And wisdom flowed from the elder.

The victim's sweet, crying voice evolved—not over a period of millions of years—to a lashing tongue. 'He is the father of my child . . .' She shifted her chair further than her rear end and stood up, but when she did so, the chair flipped! 'I do not need your judgment, damn it,' she said indignantly. 'I need someone to listen . . . to understand!' And she walked off, leaving her steaming words of insult behind.

My expectation that the discussion would result in a solution did not materialize. The victim simply wanted attention in order to feel better. First I had encountered a lady who did not need to hear the cost of perfume, and now Mrs Victim refused to consider a suggestion of divorce.

So, I finished my drink and went to do some window shopping. Soon I encountered a large business entrance—a hardware store and do-it-yourself centre. A big man at the door was waving his arms. He was red in the face and spat words of condemnation to a woman who seemed to be his own age. 'He's my son, but by God, I will kill him! He told me he would rather use dagga and coke than attend university and take over this business. You better talk to that son of yours! I have had enough of him!'

'Calm down . . . just calm down! You will pop a vein,' his wife pleaded, having followed him out of the store.

It was Chequebook Lady from the pharmacy! He was not fighting about the cheque. She would probably be able to calm him down if he had complained. Or had she done that already?

'He must become something in life!' Cranky Dad declared. 'Were is Craig now?'

Craig suddenly exited the store now, and entered the discussion: 'I will be what I want to become, and not what anyone in the family or at school wants me to become!' He walked away quickly.

'Where are you going, Craig?' his mother asked, her concerned quite evident.

'Going home and then ice skating,' he said as he watched his dads' movements.

'You dare not use the car my, boy!' his dad warned.

'See if I care . . . there is a bus you know.' He kicked one of the cement bags on display outside the sore and ran away.

Chequebook Lady looked my way. 'Are you buying something?' she asked. She must have recognized me.

'Ah . . . no . . . no I am not.' And then I removed myself from the premises.

I'd had an interesting tour of the upper-class suburb. First I'd encountered Chequebook Lady, then Mrs Victim. To crown it all, I'd learned that the son of a well-established businessman would rather turn to dagga and coke than attend university. What a discovery!

The fourth seat from the door on the bus was not my regular place, but I changed my mind this time around. A few stops later a youngster made it onto the bus just in time and breathed a sigh of relief; he placed himself on the seat opposite mine. Suddenly we recognized one another. I recalled him kicking the cement bag.

'Where do I know you from?' Craig asked, sitting upright.

'I do not know you, Craig, I—'

'You know my name. How did you get that?' he asked scratching his head.

'I noticed you kick a cement bag in front of your dad's store. I am the guy you almost ran over.' And I introduced myself.

'You're right. I thought I recognized you. So you heard my father's issues with me?'

'Yes. And it sounds the same as the one I have with my dad,' I confirmed. 'You said you would rather use dagga and coke than attend university. Is that true?' I asked concerned.

'No, that's only a way to show him I am serious. I need him to listen to me . . . I am not going to university. I am going to become a plumber by trade.'

Here was someone who really desired to be a tradesman. We got talking, and I explained how my father expected me to become a tradesman, and how, instead, I wanted to go into business with Dimitri the latest Greek owner and open a Spar food store.

'Okay this where I get off,' he said as if he was not interested in hearing my story. 'Do you hang out at the ice rink at all?'

'Yes. Not today, I am working in the shop.'

'Good, then I will see you there sometime. Good luck on convincing your old man.' And Craig jumped off, as if the bus did not stop quickly enough for him.

Dimitri was glad to see me. 'It's my mother's birthday,' he said. 'The priest is coming over. I will see you by nine thirty tomorrow tonight, okay?'

'Okay,' I replied. 'I have discussed the Spar possibility with my father, and he is not happy.'

'Ha . . . leave it to me. I will discuss it with him. I am sure he wants you to do well in life,' Dimitri said and excused himself.

So, I opened the doors for business on Sunday morning. I would serve and see to the running of the shop. I was very excited, and I had a spring in my step. As I was preparing for the day, Anita's mother ran in. 'I need milk . . . Hurry! Come on hurry!'

'Good morning, Mrs Meyer. How is everyone?' I enquired.

'If everything was well, young man, I would not be here for milk so that Anita could rinse her stomach!'

'Rinse her stomach . . . but why, Mrs Meyer?' I noticed by now the panic of a desperate mother.

'Overdose. Do not look at me like that, young man. And all that for a man. No man is worth that. All you men are the same,' she said and threw the money on the counter.

'Did you call for an ambulance?'

'No! What she needs is a good hiding!' And off she went.

I did not hesitate. I recalled Anita's passionate characteristic way of conducting herself. I called the emergency services. *Her green eyes shouldn't go dull*, I thought to myself. *They have to stay alive.*

Soccer players and spectators flooded the shop. At eleven o'clock, Mrs Meyer appeared at the door again. 'Who gave you the right to call for the ambulance? Who do you think you are, God's gift to humanity? Let me remind you, you're not our type and will never be!' She was spitting her heart out at me.

'You know what, madam?' This voice came out of nowhere. It was the voice of a domestic worker. 'My daughter died because we did not get her to hospital in time. My husband blames me, but he did nothing when I cried about my baby being sick. Your child is alive—'

'I do not need a domestic's comment, thank you,' Mrs Meyer interrupted with a 'you-are-beneath-me' attitude.

Then Mr. Meyer appeared behind his wife. 'Ignore my wife please,' he said to me. 'Thank you, Alwyn, and for whatever it may mean to you, I was wrong about you.' Mr Meyer bravely spoke, and then dragged his wife home.

Reality returned with the sudden realization that 'my shop' was packed with customers—all waiting. My excitement and energy could not come to a halt as I pictured myself as a future co-owner of the local Spar. I was pumped—until Dimitri walked in at closing time.

Cashing up had me concerned again. Dimitri and I were going to talk to Dad. Would Dad be willing for me to be a businessperson . . . a co-owner?

We knocked, we were welcomed in, and we asked for Dad's undivided attention. In a friendly way, he granted it.

Dimitri gave good reasons, explaining why the partnership would succeed. He tendered a whole business plan, with contracts that were legally binding. 'Mr Van, your son is the person we want in our business. We believe he is the right person to train and have as co-owner.'

'My son must first become a man; he needs to do his military service first. Anyway, the army has called him up for two years, and he cannot get out of it.'

'Mr Van, we have investigated the matter. We will apply for exemption on account of his being a partner and businessman.' Dimitri was negotiating. 'He will make a good living for himself. Please allow Alwyn the chance of a lifetime.'

'I have two sons, and there will be no "rich man—poor man" playoff between two brothers,' Father insisted.

Dimitri stopped with a shocked expression on his face.

Mother tried: 'Van, I will look after our son's interests while he is in uniform. It is a great opportunity for him. I am sure Dimitri will not mind.'

'His brother hates working in the shop,' said Dimitri. 'And he has other talents. Alwyn has worked for a long period in the shop, and we know what he is like. Allow him the opportunity, please.' Dimitri did not want to give up.

'He will go and do a trade,' my persistent father went on. 'There is security in a trade.' 'Tradesmen do not earn a lot of money unless they have their own business, sir. We will teach him all about the business. Mr Van, please don't throw the opportunity away.'

'He is under twenty-one and will do as I tell him. He is not of age; therefore, I will give consent as and when I see fit,' Father replied.

'Mr Van, please rethink your decision. It's a life-changing opportunity. Take a week or two, and then we will talk again,' Dimitri suggested.

'There is nothing to think about, and that is the way it will be,' Father said, turning his back on all concerned.

Many a week went by, and Dad would not even talk about it. 'What I say is law,' he reminded me, and, 'The law gives me that power.' His power of the law had me disgusted in that law.

'If most judges were like you, the world would be corrupt, Dad.'

The 'super power' had shown his muscles and made them felt. Then he had lapsed into proud silence.

Having a Saturday afternoon off and the ice rink as a social 'getaway' destination, I looked forward to mingling with some of my friends. Craig was there with many a friend. He totally ignored me, and we enjoyed our evenings in separate groups.

'I thought I may find you here, Alwyn.' A very familiar voice declared her presence. She had always been a lovely girl; now she was becoming a stunning young woman. Mary Orphan caused a lot of heads to turn.

'I am glad to see you here,' I said, trying to maintain a happy mood.

'I need an escort, for there are too many arrogant boys.' After a few minutes, she said, 'So come out with it, and speak your mind.'

I sidestepped her questions.

'You never burden others with your issues, Alwyn. For so many years you have heard me out and you have always been there for me. This time I insist—share your heart.'

Mary Clark looked at me with eyes that I knew I could trust. There are few people in the world we can share things with . . . open our hearts to.

Mary and I had always shared every detail of our lives. As always, there was a feeling of vitalizing the power we shared. This is a commodity seldom found.

Suddenly Craig made his appearance. His friendly demeanour was in overdrive, and his smile was larger than Africa itself. He talked to me about how he got what he wanted—how his 'Chartered Accountant' Aunt convinced his father, and how he would have a supplier in his dad for all his plumbing requirements. Simultaneously, he could not take his eyes of Mary Clark.

'I will be a businessman of stature,' Craig told us. Then turned to me. 'Your old man, did he live up to it?' But, he did not wait for my response. He simply commanded me, 'Introduce me to Miss South Africa, will you?' What a pick-up line.

'Yes, this is Craig and . . .'

Mary stepped forward ' . . . and Miss South Africa.' Craig swallowed his tongue, and Mary continued, 'Now, if you will excuse the two of us, we're in the middle of something important. Will you now?' She turned to me, took hold of my hand, and asked me to lead her onto the ice.

With blades on the icy surface, she was skating in reverse. Mary then pleaded with me. 'Don't ever become an arrogant bastard, please . . .'

'Are you *expecting* that from me?' I asked concerned.

'No . . .' She lifted her head and gave me her characteristic smile. ' . . . or I'll kick your shin! Please, don't become what you're not.'

Is man thy tool of destruction or thy source of begetting? —Wynie

13

Hope or suggested death penalty?

I had no option than being obedient to my father's wishes. I became a tradesman. The military called me up for two year service. In that period in uniform I made friends with a most beautiful young lady. Yes we were young but I gave my heart to her.

Jane's father, as in the case of Anita's mother objected to our relationship. He did not believe that a man for 'Sodom and Gomorra' – referring to Johannesburg—would be from the desired social setting for his daughter. In September of that year Jane's father's words was clearly stated 'What good can come out of Mayfair? Without judging you, you will not meet the standard I demand for my daughter.'

I had to abandon the hopeless situation, leaving my heart on the floor. Trampled.

Through friends I was introduced to a woman, Janeen who became my wife. Yes the names Jane and Janeen were similar. My feelings for Jane I most probably transferred to Janeen and may have been to young to realise.

I later found that she was engaged before my time. Were we on the rebound when we met? Married life had 'little communication and action by assumption' only.

Obstacles surely followed.

In the later part of 1989, I, at thirty years young, had once again so much to live for. I had a good life with miles ahead to look forward to – or so I thought. The beginning of life and living life had its natural cause. As for the end of life, I had my mind made up that life comes and life goes in many a form. I might have been too logical about it.

However, I had gone through the firsthand experience of a dreaded disease in my young married days. In our third year of marriage, in 1984, a doctor broke the news to us that my young wife had cancer. She was twenty-four at the time.

After surgery and all the emotions related to it, radiation was the only option. From sixty-three kilograms, she disappeared to a mere forty-one kilograms. Treatment was Monday to Friday, and travelling that distance every day, and having to take time off from work, became strenuous to my occupation as a Draughtsman,

At times treatment would not be possible because of having a blood condition, so days would go by and she would feel miserable. The fear of dying pushed to the surface. We questioned the professor on the matter. Very quickly and rudely, he failed in trying to get her 'out of denial' as he put it.

My expectation was that he could have done something about her blood condition. I told him, 'I am a practical man. If you are sure that chemotherapy and radiation are positive treatments, you should have enough experience to do something about her blood condition.'

I was 'below his class', and he spoke as if he knew where the line of life and death was, and we needed to respect his call. I noticed he was not focused on his work that day; his mind was wandering, and his irises were high in their sockets, as if in a dormant stare.

She was crying, upset, so I had to do something, and I did. Outside the allopathic profession, we found a solution for her blood condition, and the radiation was successfully completed. Prior to that, I had suggested this particular solution to him, but he would hear nothing of it. So here again, pretence had to have a front seat in order to find a healthy destination.

The experience had me, as the young husband, in many a tumultuous moment, with my mind constantly adjusting. The pretence of the healthy partner that all is well in a relationship that is strained by a disease, can be extremely exhausting to that healthy partner.

As a young married man, limited and implemented self-restriction, withholding, for not violating the consent of needy romantic action. Noting her guilty expression for not complying with my expectations, I learned that our individual needs were not of the same season. Five years went by without our seasons meeting, for her winter would come to my summer, and my spring appeared in her autumn.

My community service was a life-sharing experience, whereby I maintained my sanity. It was an escape from my circumstantial reality. Margret Smith, a social worker, had a request she asked me to think about it. 'My father in-law is dying, and the whole family is falling apart. My concern is that he does not speak about it. His children do not visit him as regularly as they should. They say he avoids them. Please talk to him; I'd rather have him die in peace.'

'I do not know this man,' I countered. 'How can I just enter the home and mend—'

'You have a talent and a gift.' Her green eyes opened wider, as if to say, 'You won't have a problem.' When she spoke again, she said, 'I will make the appointment with my mother-in-law and confirm. Okay?'

'Okay.' My mind now was wondering about her desperation. 'I will await your confirmation.'

That evening I lay wide awake. I was twenty-one when my father died. I still remember the evening my father did not come home at the usual time. Then out of nowhere, the police service radio announced that a tragic accident had happened. I walked out of the house as a police officer approached the front door. 'Did your father drive a Hillman Vogue?' he asked.

The officer had started his statement with *did* and not *does*. I knew we would never see him again. He left it up to the station commander to tell me over the phone.

No warning in advance, an accident. 'Just accept it?' No matter how sad one is, nothing one can say or do could give back life. Often Father would request, 'The good die young, and when that happens, then leave me in peace.'

Now I had to go and talk to Dave, a dying man—a man who knew he was dying.

Two or three days later that week, we knocked on the door. His wife opened, and her face mirrored sadness. Her eyes were a revelation of sleepless nights. She spoke softly, trying to spare his ears from the depressing wording shared under their roof as if protecting his feelings. I requested we all visit around his bed, and so we did.

After the introduction, we talked about a few commonplace things. I paid attention to his participation; he seemed to enjoy it. His wife looked more comfortable and used the 'do you remember Dad' phrase. Those few minutes went quickly.

Uncle Dave and I looked at one another, and a few seconds felt like minutes. He smiled with expectation of where the visit could lead. My smile conveyed, *It's all right.*

'Uncle Dave, is it fine with you if we talk about the fact of dying?'

His wife and daughter-in-law were hysterical by my request—and his consent. They excused themselves. 'We are going to make something to drink,' his wife said as they hurried out of the room.

'Let them go,' he said. 'Pretending is tiring.'

'Pretending?'

'Yes. They expect me to believe—or think—that I will live for a few years more. I want them to accept the reality.'

'That cannot be easy, can it?' I asked.

'It is not easy for anyone of us, I know,' Uncle Dave agreed. 'I understand there is a need to deal with emotions, but I need them to know that I'm alive for now. I need quality time with them.' He paused for several minutes.

'When they stand around me with that 'what a shame . . . look at him' expression on their faces and make gestures of full-blown sympathy, I feel that my life has no meaning at all.'

We did not utter a word for at least three minutes. I noted that tears formed in the corners of his eyes. 'I know I am leaving this life, and I am ready for the next,' he told me. 'Does that answer your question?'

'Ready?' I said. 'And—'

He interrupted me. 'Let my children know that I have made the decision to accept whatever comes my way, for I have left it in God's hands.'

Uncle Dave went silent as his wife entered the room, but I was sure her ears had picked up his last sentence. We enjoyed coffee while we talked about their children and grandchildren. Uncle Dave and I made frequent eye contact; I noticed how he looked at his wife with a tender glance. His eyes carried a message of love. She noticed. Then it was time to leave. I told them that I was on my way.

'Will you pray for us before leaving?' Uncle Dave made this request with positive expectation.

'Off course,' I agreed.

He reached for my hand. 'Pray for my family rather than for me,' his eyes insisted, and we did.

We said goodbye. 'Let them know about my decision,' he reminded me. 'Some day they will understand.'

Driving home, I wondered about the way a doctor might inform a patient about imminent death. Was there a way that could instil hope rather than simply a death penalty?

Uncle Dave was laid to rest a few weeks later.

———————————————

It may be good to avoid controversy and subtle damnation spoken unto them, suspended between life and death. —Wynie

14

Fool is he . . . unto whom?'

Sanctions, economics, politics, and sport boycotts dominated the media in the 1980s. Hope and doom were the emotional shapers that inspired human behaviour to reach to a variety of actions as people searched for some kind of 'happy place'.

The engineering industries were influenced by a shortage of industrial implements and capital equipment. Focused on designing, and being part of a team in a manufacturing company, I, like most others, endured my own hiccups and 'life sanctions'.

We were in the process of adopting and fostering children. My wife could not bear children, because she had radiation therapy that followed a hysterectomy, and she felt a pressing need to be a mother.

My life's game was spoiled. It felt as if there was no redeemer anywhere again, and it was difficult not to 'make war in the mind'.

My wife was still recuperating, and this was accompanied by intense anxiety over adopting, for our youthful expectations did not have all the joy that belongs to most young lovers.

Life seemed normal for everyone around me at work until the morning the engineer interviewed a woman who caught the attention of every eye she passed by. Wearing long slacks and high-heeled shoes, she marched by as if on a modelling parade, for someone might fancy her sense of fashion—and many did.

One engineer, Edward, opened the door and showed her in. Her bow, suggestive of humility, had his eyes nailed to her buttocks. After he unsuccessfully reached for the door handle for the third time, he was obliged to release his eyes from her form and close the door.

As the trailer will follow the horse, Hendry, the costing manager, had been only a few steps behind. 'The best butt I've ever seen,' he called out to the rest of us, with his mind fixed on something only he could imagine.

Hendry then walked into my office. 'Man, what must a man do to get into her space?'

'Probably ask her permission,' I said sarcastically.

Hendry looked at his co-worker with wonder in his eyes. 'I hope Edward employs her in a hurry.'

'Get out of here. Don't you have work to do?'

'Hold me back,' he said, laughing. 'Just hold me back, for I need her in my space.'

'Then use the other door so your temptation won't be so intense,' I commanded.

The following week she walked in with handbag and briefcase, and her attitude invaded the office. Sandra-Lee had arrived! Everyone knew what she wanted; we got the message: 'I am professional, and I either work or play. When I am here, I work; when I am out of here, I play as I please. I do a good job either way.'

I was summonsed to Hendry's office after a few weeks of peace and hard work. Here life would offer up yet another 'office twist' that would bear down like a volcano waiting to burst out of its crust.

Would one expect humans to act responsibly when disaster reveals its cause?

As I entered Hendry's office, he said, 'Close the door behind you, Alwyn . . . please!'

I hesitated. 'Sounds like you have bad news—or do I sense gossip surfacing from among the men?'

'Just close the door, damn it. Please.' It was an order.

'What's on your mind? Why do you need to see me?'

Hendry lay back in his chair as if enjoying his La-Z-Boy. 'Can you keep a secret?'

'Why? Do you know of a pay rise coming?'

'No, man, I am in love!' He sat up as if needing to whisper in my ear. 'I am in love . . . for the first time I have lost it!'

'Lost it?' I enquired.

'She is sexy . . . she is beautiful . . . she makes my blood warm . . . she's got it. I am falling for her!' Hendry sang her praises.

'Falling for her and you've lost your mind? What's up?'

'I need you to be quiet about it. I need you to solemnly promise!'

'What comes over your lips in this office will remain in this office.'

'Good. I have a date with Sandra-Lee this weekend.'

'First time, and you are in love? Come on!' I tried the 'wake-up' call. I stood up. 'Now you have to excuse me. I have work to do.' I closed the door behind me on my way out.

A few metres before turning into my office, Sarah, the tea-girl, approached me. 'Alwyn, how is your wife's heath these days?' We chatted for a short while. She expressed concern about her sister's health. She asked me for advice about how to handle the situation. Sandra-Lee appeared from nowhere.

'If you need advice, Sarah,' she said, 'talk to someone who knows.' She gave me an attacking stare like that of a Doberman. She was a female dog aiming for a response. 'The only thing he can do properly is draw a few lines on paper showing others how to make things and put them together.'

'Sarah, I will talk to you in the canteen at lunchtime, okay?' I suggested, and we walked off with Doberman standing in solitary fury, showing a canine or two.

The weekend came and went. It was Monday morning, and I arrived at work early. I looked out the window to see a strange car stop at the gate. A woman in the passenger seat was kissing a man in the driver's seat. He was hanging on for dear life. Who could that be?

Standing closer to the window, I was amazed to see a passion playoff. Okay! What a revelation! Doberman got out of the car, looked around, and then trod to the driver's door, bent down, and showed the stallion what was waiting for him.

Sandra-Lee walked into the office, dropped her bag on her desk, and prepared coffee. Hendry then walked in, opened his door, placed his briefcase on his desk, and went up to her as if some hormone in the air had magnetic power upon him.

From where I sat, my view through an open door revealed something similar to an overactive Jack Russell terrier seeking the attention from his mistress. But all he got was coffee and an instruction to have it in his office. And so he did.

At lunchtime I had to hear the 'report back' complaints from a not-so-enthusiastic Hendry. He described her home, furnished with the most expensive interior and photos of vacations and boat cruises. This life style was not new to me for she was the topic of gossip among the lady's in office.

'Your in-love status seems to be changed,' I probed.

'It seemed to go well until her 'beeper' rudely interrupted our visit. She went off and got to a phone as quickly as possible. On returning she said I would have to excuse her in about thirty minutes, as she needed to go and 'help out' a friend.'

'Beeper . . . help a friend . . . like a doctor on call?' I was amazed.

'She said she would make it up to me if I'd just understand.' Hendry sounded uncertain.

I shared my concerns with Hendry about Sandra-Lee's high standard of living while earning only a limited basic salary—the motorcar she drove, the home she lived in, the clothing she wore, and the expensive get-aways. 'Her social life by far exceeds her budget,' I concluded.

'What are you suggesting, Alwyn? That she's a two-dollar prostitute?' He was very upset of course.

'The occasional two dollars would not provide her that type of lifestyle.'

'She's not like that.' And Hendry excused himself.

On my way to the gents one afternoon after clock-out time, I wondered if my eyes deceived me or not; for here, about fifteen metres ahead, Edward and Sandra-Lee were walking out of the ladies' bathroom. *Am I seeing things?* I wondered.

Confused, I entered the gents' toilet. The sales manager was washing hands, so I asked him when he last had seen Edward the engineer. I was not surprised to hear his answer: 'This morning in a board meeting. Now I have just arrived from a full day with clients.'

Hendry somehow heard the gossip that Edward and Sandra-Lee had been seen making their way out of the ladies' bathroom. The gossip increased and caused embarrassing moments for the two of them when the financial manager saw them kissing.

'Jack Russell Hendry' was now on the witch hunt, following Sandra-Lee wherever she went after work. One evening he used his brother's car and followed her to a five-star hotel. She parked her Alfa and got into an expensive German car. He followed them for some distance to another five-star hotel, and into the building where they entered the restaurant for dinner.

After dinner, they took the escalator up to the second floor. Hendry realized it too late and could not follow at a close distance in order to learn what room they would be using for her evil deeds. Edward was not the man she was kissing—or now . . .

The following morning Hendry opened his heart to me. He told me how he had hoped for the two of them to be together, if only she would give him a chance. She told him that he was the marrying type—a good type—and she would commit to loving a man like him—one day.

Having high hopes, and being blinded by infatuation, his reasoning was absent. Jack Russell Hendry had his tail up again, and Doberman Sandra-Lee did not mind, for then Edward would not find out and ask unwanted questions.

I had the need to discuss important matters with Hendry and knocked on his office door. No answer. I tried to open it so I could leave him a note. The door was locked—without a 'do not disturb' sign.

Then I entered the stationary storeroom, and just before leaving, I heard Jack Russell's office door open. Walking around the corner, I found Doberman in the doorway about to leave. She smiled back into the room with a face that conveyed 'I have licked your wounds, have I?' and left Jack Russell sitting.

I went into the office. 'It's not like you, Hendry, to just sit behind your desk when someone enters or leaves.' I was being sarcastic. I gave him my request regarding manufacturing necessities.

At the door, I turned to Hendry. 'Please straighten your belt and trousers before leaving your office.' He could only blush.

Thursday at teatime, Hendry walked into my office with his tail between his legs. It was not the lousy pay increase that had him in a state. His head hung as if he had lost his superior position to a new leader of the pack.

I stopped in front of him 'Who stole your bone?'

'She is going on a hiking trip with some friends,' he said, sulking.

'Hiking?

Hendry tried to hide his anger, frustration, and disparateness. Then, with fists closed halfway, making them look like claws looking for something to tear apart, he exhibited his emotion. 'How do I get her to stay in *my* space, Alwyn?'

Then again, I had my own frustrations and life sanction held against me. At times my restlessness desired a direction that could allow me to commit emotional release with a woman willing to have no commitment . . . no strings attached. One calls it adultery.

'Hendry, I am in a space where I am frustrated. Will you not avoid consolatory confinement imposed upon yourself?' I almost pleaded.

'Man I am not like you. If she allows me, she will never look at another,' he explained.

'Hendry, it is relationship suicide to get into or stay in a dying relationship,' I pleaded again.

'You're not a preacher, so stay out of my mind!' Hendry left in a hurry.

One weekend I had to work. I was surprised to see Edward's wife in his office. Edward was nowhere to be seen. 'Edward is showing a good example, getting his wife to do his admin work,' I said to her. I was looking for conversation.

'He called me and asked me to pick up a file he needed to study for Monday morning's meeting,' she said, smiling. 'And no, his attorney wife will not do his admin. It's for that reason he employed Sandra-Lee. See?' she said with authority.

'Sounds like he's gone for the weekend?' I probed suspiciously.

'Hiking with friends as usual, out in the mountains.'

'Do you go hiking with him at times?' I wondered.

'Once, yes, a few years ago. No! That's not for this lady, thank you.' She left the office.

That would not be a coincidence, now would it? Okay, assumption is a dangerous thing. However, put yourself in my shoes. Would you not have made a calculated assumption? Is the human mind not endowed with the capacity to discriminate? Would it be judgemental to label another as judgemental? Think so?

Hendry was making war in his mind. He went into surveillance mode with imagination and a healthy creative suspicion. He acquired tolerance in keeping himself sane. Binoculars and scope provided an ambushed view. Yes! At least half an hour after sunset, the Audi stopped in front of Sandra-Lee's home.

'Last night I saw it all!' Hendry's chin dropped towards his chest.

Here was a man who had experienced a great loss. Hendry's expectations had been hijacked and ambushed by circumstances and others' choices. Then suddenly a fighting spirit entered the broken man. 'His wife needs to know. I will see to that,' he bravely said.

'No! You will not,' I reprimanded him 'You do not know their circumstances.'

'So what do you know about his circumstances? Are you defending him? Are you justifying Sandra-Lee's behaviour?' Hendry was furious.

'No I'm not,' I explained in a quiet manner. 'It's . . . something I have considered as well.'

'What are you on about?' Hendry showed empathy.

'At times I would not have minded to have had a Sandra-Lee in my life. You know my circumstances at home, and I understand. It is difficult for a woman who had lost her life-giving faculties to get in the right frame of mind, or so the doctor explained.'

'Are you saying that Edward is in the same situation?' Hendry pulled his shoulders in question.

'No. I'd like you to keep it to yourself, for you do not know what goes on within the four walls of their home.'

Two weeks later the staffs' Christmas banquet was held. Everyone—or almost everyone—walked in with a spouse or partner.

Hendry and I sat there without partners. 'Here's Sandra-Lee walking in with her five-star male escort,' Hendry described in a broken voice.

'Was it not good for my colleague to have had his eyes opened in such a cruel way?'

Hendry turned to me. 'You have a partner . . . a wife. Did she not come along because she is ill? Or did she not come out of choice?'

As Hendry waited for a response, he found me staring into an unseen dimension. 'Alwyn, how often would you not have minded . . . to have had a Sandra-Lee in your life?'

I felt my eyes tearing up, and then held back a flood that could confirm my frustrations. 'I had the opportunity not too long ago. Guilt helped me drive the temptation away.'

'What a fool you—' then Hendry was interrupted by someone else briefly.

'Fool am I?' I responded. 'To whom? At times I am glad I did not . . . and yet most of the time I stare at the ceiling, angry at myself, for I have lost out on something that might have been great.' My eyes then moved back to the unseen.

'You are losing out now . . .' Hendry looked around. 'Your wife is nowhere to be seen.'

I sighed deeply. 'Hendry, at times I do not know, and today I cannot tell you what her motives would be.'

'Alwyn . . . that's not living life,' he said with concern.

'So I am a foolish man . . . to whom?'

Is sympathy and loving kindness not nourishment unto those who are close to you? —Wynie

15

Love's connection, disconnected

Life is the most wonderful gift. You may have had the privilege of carrying life within the womb for nine months, or even to a healthy premature arrival. How many times will one burst with joy after delivering a baby into this world?

Just imagine you are in an airplane. It then transforms into a time machine and takes you from one era to another. You are invited to fasten your seatbelts, sit at ease, and you may need a tissue.

We move over a distance of twenty years. On landing, you're at the door of a family glad to receive you, for the hour of inspiration is welcome.

Seven-year-old Suzan was sitting on the carpet, legs folded. In front of her on the floor was an open Bible. I had just shared a short story with a lesson of faith with Suzan and her younger sibling, who was sitting on their mother's lap. Daddy oversaw everything with a face that expressed a very satisfied mood.

Suzan responded with excitement, 'My teacher told me the same story!' She bubbled with joy seldom seen in this degree of spiritual maturity. 'Uncle Alwyn I love God and I love Jesus and . . .' she expressed her heart-felt conviction.

How honest can a child be at this age? Would one question her perception of love? I would not dare to. Her parents were proud of their daughter's sincerity, and her good influence that grew from it.

Back home, I entered my children's room, kissed their cheeks, and whispered. 'I love you . . . good night,' in their ears. At the same time, I saw to it that they were covered properly.

The next week after Suzan listened to the story, she asked about angels and how they would carry people to heaven. Then she asked if she could pray. She did, and not for herself however; it was short and to the point.

Her mother then stated a concern: 'I have noticed some changes on Suzan. Her teacher also shared concern about the fact that Suzan was growing hair all over. It may be a hormone problem,' she said.

I suggested they see the doctor who had treated my wife. That week, the doctor referred Suzan to a brain specialist. The family were traumatized when they learned that she had a brain tumour that had to be removed. It was news that echoed beyond love's connection that life could end for her.

Suzan was prepared for surgery. At visitation hour, we entered one of the most sophisticated, modern, and organized hospitals. The walls and glass were clean, the sparkle reflecting on the door handles and windows. It was all impressive, and helped us build an expectation in our minds that maybe, just maybe, a miracle would invite itself and rescue Suzan.

Her mother walked out of the ward, allowing her tears to flow freely after she had bravely held them in. Her face revealed concern, fear, and hopelessness. My attention was drawn to her eyes, which reached far beyond a stare. It was as if they were fixed on an unseen scene, after pleading for help and desperately awaiting an answer.

Her shoulders dropped as her head bowed under emotional paralysis. Mother then lifted her head as if emerging from a deep-water pool in need of a life-giving sustenance. All her facial muscles shared in the groaning sound that no parent ever wants to experience. She placed a note in my hand.

I read it, and handed it back to her. She held on to the note for dear life, then looked at me. Her eyes closed as exhaustion overtook her strength. She sat down, and it was evident that hopelessness was knocking at her heart.

'What does the note say?' someone asked in anticipation.

With a lump in my throat, 'Your God . . . is my God . . . where you go . . . I shall go . . .' Then there was a silence no one dared to interrupt.

Suzan's father, locked in a state of shock, floated in the 'zombie-syndrome' as I walked next to him. There was silence between us. We knew that words would not change the emotion. A tsunami of fear flooded the father's soul as circumstances were out of his control. Having had a glimpse of my own tsunami, I could understand his emotional turmoil.

Many seasons ago from that day, my recollection was clear. 'Alwyn, your wife has an aggressive cancer. We might take the chance and allow her to go through with a pregnancy, however it would be dangerous,' the professor had said without uncertain terms.

That statement caused me to feel as if my life-giving properties were being withheld from me. Will my wife live? Will I ever have the privilege to conceive a child? Would the gift of 'love's life' be withheld from me forever?

Suzan words, 'Your God . . . is my God . . . where you go . . . I shall go . . .' directed my mind to another of her statements: 'Uncle . . . I love God . . . Jesus and . . .' This captivated my thoughts for a long time.

That evening I turned and tossed, got out of bed, and visited my children's room. They were sleeping peacefully. The next morning they would wake up, and we would be living in grace. For Suzan, however, I was not sure. Would she awake to a normal life after this major surgery? Would she live? The grace of God was the only thing I could pray for.

Three traumatic days passed by, and Suzan was in a coma. She did not awake to a normal life. In fact, everyone had to accept the fact—overnight—that Suzan would not resurrect out of the coma. Her mother and father were broken parents, emotionally paralyzed, for one of their life connections had been disconnected.

My need of a 'life connection' had been boycotted, withheld, by circumstances. For many days, I would wonder about the gift of life and the passing on of it from one generation to another. Suzan's short life history was only a short story that influenced many lives.

And so Suzan was relocated from the sophisticated hospital of the northern suburbs to the public hospital in the south. I walked up the stairs and asked directions to her room. I was led to her bedside. We walked from a colourful, life-promising ward to an empty 'place of safety' where she was held. Not a soul was in close proximity to this unused ward. I turned to the nurse 'Does anyone watch over her?'

'She does not need much, sir. You do understand.' And she made her way out as fast as possible.

I was there with a lifeless girl and the sound of 'Umm . . . umm . . .' On and on and again: 'Umm . . . umm . . .' She was mumbling! I was shocked at where I had found her. I walked back to the door in search of a staff member, for I had questions, and I needed answers.

When I got to the door, she was quiet. I stopped and turned back to Suzan. When I walked back to her motionless being, her mumbling started again. I talked to her, and I saw movement. With major effort, she was making her muscles contract, suggesting the need of the foetal position. I spoke to her. Her mumbling sounded as if she was acknowledging what I was saying.

I placed her hand in my hand; it was small and weak, and I wondered how many times Suzan's mother and father had held her hands after her birth and experienced the miracle of movement, of life. Her voice quieted down as I prayed, 'Oh, God, please have mercy upon your child . . .' I could only dream and hope for the day the Angel of Life would take hold of her hand.

After a few seconds of silence, she continued mumbling. In my mind, her words echoed again, 'Your God . . . is my God . . . where you go . . . I shall go . . . I love God . . . Jesus and . . .' and I could not control my tears again.

I found myself again unlocking my car. I could only hope that God would intervene.

The weeks passed by, and I took every opportunity possible among daily responsibilities to visit Suzan. Here again 'do not make war in your mind' was the reminder to preserve sanity. Standing next to her bed, I once again noticed something about her mumbling. This time it was as if 'peace' had entered the room.

There was a sad calmness that overcame me. Where it came from I did not understand. The nursing sister stood a few meters behind me. Then she came close to me. 'We do not think she will make morning,' she said with all the empathy in the world. I could only nod in acknowledgement; my tongue would not move. Somehow, I knew.

'You're one of the few people who come here . . . she must be special to you,' she said. 'I'll give you a few minutes before attending to her.' And she removed herself.

I held Suzan's hand as I prayed. It felt unnecessary, as if a request had been granted. It would be last time, I knew. I said goodbye with the hope of the grace of God. Then it happened. Was it my imagination, or had I felt movement in her hand?

That evening I had the need to share my experience with my wife. She did not hear a word. She turned away and fell asleep. She had probably had a difficult day, feeling ill again, and without strength. I would never know.

Then I slipped back into my shoes, went into the kitchen, and made Milo. I had a conversation with the only mind I knew—myself. It was all I had. So many times I was alone in my own world, for under my roof there was no soul that would offer a listening ear. How long would I have to endure this 'relationship suicide' or stay in a dying relationship? Would there be a cure some day?

For what was supposed to be my love connections had been disconnected. A sense of being cut off from the normal world overpowered me. Was there no redeemer anywhere for this relationship?

At four in the morning, my wife came to me. 'You need not sleep on the couch. Come to bed,' she said. Again I was facing the ceiling wondering about a dying relationship and the want of a love connection. Was a similar thing happening to Suzan's parents?

A few hours later the phone rang, and what was expected was confirmed. This time I offered no tears. I was labelled as 'cold and showing no feelings.'

Suzan was laid to rest after a few days. At the graveside, I had a back row position, and the echo in my mind remained: 'Your God . . . is my God . . . where you go . . . I shall go . . . I love God . . . Jesus and . . .' and somehow I was at peace.

I then turned to a friend next to me. 'Some short-life stories are more powerful than he who reasons with wisdom,' I said, and I walked way, leaving the others to pay their last respects.

Is life not a journey filled with sanctifying opportunity? —Wynie

16

What did the wives expect?

My voluntary community welfare and healthcare service was a great mental therapy that preserved my sanity. For me, my love connection had been disconnected not by death, but rather by a love life disaster that had rendered it impossible for my wife and I to pass our gift of life to a next generation.

I was interested in alternative medicine, and so I continued and enjoyed my collage studies in that discipline. So, understandingly, my wife found a new life partner who could identify with her and share the type of life she desperately needed.

Placing my energy and talents in serving the community around me amplified my desire to have an offspring of my own. For now, I was hoping that a new life lay ahead of me.

Saying goodbye to field of engineering, I took a 180-degree turn in order to focus entirely on alternative medicine.

When I was not studying, I found myself working in a pharmacy. The work itself was somewhat similar to the work I had done in shop where I used to work, yet there was a major difference. The pharmacy was often crowded, mostly with young moms. For them natural substances were the preference of the day. They were very interested in complementary medicine.

'Year in and year out, members of my family have sinus problems, and it doesn't end,' a concerned mother told me. 'Is there any way out of our predicament?'

'I believe there is,' I responded, and my attention was drawn to the close resemblance between the mother and her daughters. They were similar in structure as well as in the colour and shape of their eyes and their pale, transparent skin. The inner rim of their irises were surrounded with diamond-like beads, shining with hypnotic effect on others. Their full lips suggested their ability to communicate feeling.

I contemplated on this. 'Are you there? Hello!' She brought me out of my deep thought. 'We were referred to you, and need your assistance please.'

'Of course, please forgive me, but your daughters are carbon copies of you. How long has the sinus problem been with you?'

'Ever since I can remember, but more so since I got married and moved to Johannesburg, and my daughters started at the age of three,' the mom explained. 'And we are fed the same medication all the time. They are nine and seven years old now,' she concluded.

Happy with her visit to the pharmacy and the complementary support, the mother was positive about their future health. She recommended many others to follow her example. However, her husband was too much of a 'tough boy' for her liking.

It was a busy Saturday morning. Requests and demands were the order of the day. I noticed a reserved Japanese woman standing to one side, awaiting her opportunity. Then she disappeared, but she appeared again.

I walked up to her, and before I could pose a question, she said, 'I want a baby,' in a soft and unsure tone.

'You want what, madam?' Had I heard her correctly? 'Repeat again, please.'

'I need to have a baby.' Her shoulders dropped, and her head followed. I noticed her urgency. Here before me was a woman who was on the brink of giving up hope.

'Then, madam,' I smiled and clasped my hands together, 'I must advise you to "consult" your husband.'

Her face lit up and life returned to her voice. 'You think . . .'

'O yes, she did.' A proud man stood closer and put his arm around her. 'I assure you, and much more than once.'

'I've been all over, and have had many tests done,' she explained. 'It's about three years now.' Her despondency returned. 'I do not know what to do next.'

'The doctor said they cannot find any reason why my wife cannot conceive.' This husband was more than proud in assisting his wife in the task of conceiving their firstborn.

This Japanese couple became dead silent. They pinned their eyes on me, as if to say 'we're listening'. I notice that the dark continental iris and sclera of her eyes had a dull look. Then I inquired about her menstrual history.

After a lengthy discussion she said, 'One gynaecologist said that the condition of my uterus is such that it cannot be a fertile host.' She seemed not to understand; I heard the need for evidence.

'Then I need to repeat the following statement,' I told her. 'There is no healing without cleaning.' I handed her a tissue. 'And there *is* another thing,' I said to her. 'I would like you to be aware of carrying with you a sense of wellbeing. Do not expect a condemning sentence. Do you think you can do that?'

With hope and a new outlook on her health, she turned to me. 'So do you have hope for me then?'

I smiled. 'The hope of giving life through you is what you need to focus on. Now it is not about hope for you. It is about the hope of a new life.'

Her husband put his arms around her and smiled so that his eyes narrowed to the maximum. 'We . . . we can do that,' he said and looked at her lovingly. He picked up the package and placed it in his wife's hands. 'This was a fruitful morning, wouldn't you say?' And there they went. Their body movements projected the transformation in their minds.

Weeks went by. Every day was full of requests for good health expectations. The 1990s brought a change in attitude about health: prevention is better than cure. The idea of taking responsibility for one's health was of the order of the day. Our Japanese couple was happy to stick to the plan and collect their complementary medication regularly over a period of mouths.

'Alwyn, I have a request. Please, before I assault my husband.' It was the mother and her lookalike daughters.

'Please, madam, we do not want to bail you out from behind bars. Let me first hear your request,' I said, wanting to know what was behind this. 'What does he do to deserve such brutal punishment?'

'He is so tough, it makes me sick. You macho men are untouchable,' she said sarcastically, giving insight into the male psyche.

'And you would like to "nurse" him, bandage his wounds?' I asked. 'You need to feel appreciated for taking special care of him?'

She first looked uncomfortable, and then stood her ground. 'Years ago, before the children, he would say how he felt, whether sick or sad. It was wonderful to experience a man who needed support and care. Even then he was still a strong and tough man. But that has disappeared now.'

'Years before the children? What to your mind would have made him refuse your pampering?' I probed.

She looked stunned for a few moments, and then said, 'He used the excuse that he must stand aside for the children's sake. I suppose they take most of my energy. Yes, he is supportive. Yes, I have neglected him but . . .' She looked at the shop entrance as her husband walked into the pharmacy.

'But what . . . ?' I asked, trying to draw it out of her.

'Here he comes now. Talk to him, please,' she softly pleaded.

Eventually I had the opportunity to speak to him. I explained to her husband how his wife needed to do the nurturing, and that she wanted to be recognized for doing it. His wife needed to see his vulnerability. I told him that he needed to accept her gift of care.

The husband and daddy did not have much to say. He merely said, 'Thank you for confirming this to me. I have pondered over it for some time. I will address the matter.' He shook my hand and excused himself. It seemed as if he had just read an article in a magazine, closed it, and walked off. I watched the family as they all stood at the pay point. When they were finished, he was the one who turned around to me and gave me a smile of acknowledgement.

Many interesting and busy weeks flew by. One day, the Japanese couple returned. Above the noise of all the discussions going on around her, with a voice pitched for making a profound statement, she stood before me with the palms of her hands open to the ceiling, as if receiving the heavenly blessing. 'I am pregnant.'

Everyone saw a woman giving a message that she was desperate to share. My heart dropped to my feet. How many times had I been desperate to hear these desired words spoken unto me? 'Darling we are going to have a baby.' Then reality drew me back to the moment. I raised my arms up as if in surrender. 'Sorry, madam. I have nothing to do with this.'

'I'm having a baby. Thank you.' Many eyes were on us by then. 'We are going to have a child.'

'Oh no, madam, I was not involved.' I said this with a smile that shared her pride.

'You are right about that one,' said her husband. 'I was more than involved.' This daddy-to-be proudly stood closer. 'Madam could not wait to share the news with you. We are happy and excited. Thanks for your assistance.'

'We have confirmation that the baby and I have a good bill of health,' she told me. This life-giving woman had a song in her voice, a tone of love and the gratitude of angels. 'And he,' she said, nodding to her husband as she praised the proud father, 'is a wonderful and patient man.'

I must admit, after they left with so much gratitude, I was somewhat jealous, and somewhat rebellious.

After lunch, a sharp voice invaded all of the audible space. 'And I sat up all evening with him. You will not believe it. Now he knows what the children and I go though.'

I found it difficult to believe what I was hearing. I stood closer.

Still commanding all of audible space the voice continued. 'He is such a baby. He is in bed, and I have to do everything for him.'

'Mrs Blake?' I interrupted the bragging gossip. 'I need to talk to you.'

I moved over to a private area, and she followed me. 'Mrs Blake, what do you want from your husband? How do you want him to behave when he is ill?'

She stood there looking like someone who had been caught red-handed after ignoring a do-not-disturb notice.

'I am doing my best you know . . . Why will you . . .'

'He never complains when you are ill,' I interrupted

She took a half step back.

'He came to see me two days ago; I insisted he see a doctor.'

'And he did,' she confirmed.

'And he is ill. Not well. You wanted to "nurse" the man, and now you are complaining about him. What do you really want from him?'

She then cried, and I handed her a tissue. 'When you feel good about treating him, it's because you have and want the privilege. It's about helping him to get better, and then you will feel good about him being healthy.'

She sat down for a few minutes as if she needed treatment for shock. 'I am realizing that I have lost that loving feeling, and I am trying to make up for it. Romantically and sensually, I have pushed him aside and blamed him for being cold while I am the guilty one,' she confessed. 'What am I going to do?'

'Talk to him. I am sure he will appreciate you for it. Come on, you can do that.'

She stood up and briskly walked away, trying to hide the tears. I felt bad about it all. *Maybe I was out of line. Just maybe*, I thought, and felt like a jerk. Two hours later the pharmacist summoned me to the phone. 'There is a lady who insists on talking to you.'

'Good afternoon?' I said in my singing voice

'I've just made an appointment with a marriage counsellor, and if need be I'll get him to the doctor. And . . . ah . . . goodbye,' she managed before she started crying again.

A few years later I had my own practice in alternative medicine as an Ethno-Med Practitioner.

Therefore, my life had been filled with a mission of facilitating people to good health and meaningful relationships. I had entered the world of complementary medicine. The rewarding experiences were many.

Will all undue anxiety not be diminished when understanding that plants do not grow by worry and conscious effort? —Wynie

17

Insecurity is getting at you

A close friend, Jonathan, agreed to meet me for drinks.

'I need a shrink,' I said, referring to the problematic relationship I found myself in.

'We have known one another for a number of years,' he told me. 'We can be shrinks for each other.'

I stated that the best way I could to explain my predicament was to tell a story that unfolded to reveal my situation.

This is the story . . .

Eldon and Alma were driving on the highway, heading home, Alma at the wheel. There was a lack of interesting conversation because their relationship needed to be resuscitated. They had been living with a definite lack of romance and mystery.

Alma did not welcome Eldon's attempts to discuss their relationship, particularly the fact that their 'love connection' could not result in any children—by her choice. Her tone of voice and her words caused his communication efforts to fly out the window.

Gathering his courage, he raised raise the topic again, mentioning that he was in a state of emotional malnutrition . . . that his hunger for the sensual dish was overdue and permanently neglected. Alma then said something that made him realize that her heart was across the border, like *Titanic*'s wreckage on the floor of the ocean.

Silence overtook any attempt at communication. Their hearts beat separately, representing their separate feelings. Alma lifted her foot slightly from the petrol. As if she had all the time in the world at her disposal, the car slowed to 'window shopping' speed as she drove along the verge.

At that point, Eldon leaned his head against the headrest and closed his eyes. All the wondering and worrying had made him very tired. He woke up as the swing of the steering wheel pulled them back on the highway. Just when his focus came back on track, a surprise statement from Alma entered the empty space. 'I would not take *him* to church.' She was referring to a sexual suggestion. Surprisingly, the sweet sound of desire changed the mood of her statement.

'Who is such a lucky man?' Eldon asked.

Alma pointed to a billboard along the highway.

'Okay! Richard Gere, the lover boy.' Eldon noted the advert of an upcoming movie. 'Have you ever had similar feelings towards a lucky man who has actually been on the receiving end?'

'Your insecurity is getting to you,' she replied with a sharp tongue and her chin in an 'up-town girl' lift. Alma shared a piece of her sober mind, for she had life's balance at her feet, any time of day.

Eldon learned that Alma would provide a spontaneous reactive defence response to any statement hinting at her spontaneous romantic reactions.

As they approach home, they passed the suburb's church on left side of the road. The naughty side of Eldon surfaced. 'There's a church! There is a church, girl! I will love you for not taking *me* to church.'

'There you go again. Your insecurity is getting to you.' This was another reactive response from a heart that was full of sound judgment—Alma's judgment. Her voice simulated a chain saw cutting down every pillar of his factual arguments. Home was only one kilometre away. Thank goodness for small mercies.

Eldon avoided discussing his desire to not use contraceptives. He desired the natural cause and effect that would result in conception and birth. Knowing that their relationship could not be mended, be it with commonsense, logic, or love, they enjoyed peace for a couple of weeks, until she made the request that he would not dare to ignore. 'You are taking me to the movies.' Alma sounded adamant.

'That sounds like an order, Your Highness,' Eldon said, hinting for a 'please!'

'Eldon, I am going to the movies, and you are taking me. And you are going to enjoy it!' This was her demand.

'Ha! I love it when a woman knows what she wants. *Ma-mama! I need a man, Put my tongue to his head spat my poison now his dead. Ma-mama*' His need for sarcastic punches was evident. Freddie Mercury and Queen would have loved the lyrics.

'I need nothing from any man,' she proudly responded.

'I am glad to hear that. So I will hunt until I find a woman in need,' he said in calm voice. 'Indeed.'

'I am in need, for you will go with me to the movie. Today!'

'Okay . . . Okay. Hallelujah I have a woman in need,' he said in mock praise.

At about six o'clock, Eldon escorted Alma to the car, opened the door for her, then got in himself and started the engine, all so that Her Highness could be driven to the cinemas. After three minutes, he broke the silence. '*Shall We Dance*? What is this movie all about? Whet my cinema appetite. Give me something to look forward to, girl.'

'Richard Gere,' she replied.

'Okay! Good. I'm starting to like the man.'

She did not hesitate. 'Mmm . . . that man is gorgeous.'

'Therefore you would not take him to church,' he said while admiring her beauty. He wondered if there was any hope for this relationship . . . if there was still any reason to stay. He was looking for solutions; all the advice of 'just love her' had not brought about a return over a period of three years.

On arriving at the cinemas, Eldon's ears were flooded with Alma's statements of heartfelt emotional fantasy, accompanied by suggestive gasps. Alma did not hold back. 'I would give him special attention anytime—if he wanted to dance, if he wanted to . . . if he wanted to . . .'

With tickets in hand, they queued to enter the cinema. Alma looked up at the 'lover boy' poster and smiled, rubbing her hands with an 'I am ready for you' gesture. They were seated; Alma leaned over and held on to Eldon's arm. She was relaxed, friendly, and patiently waiting, until the movie started.

Eldon did not mind a girly movie, and never offered an objection. He had just started to enjoy *Shall We Dance?* when the 'mmm . . . wow' sounds made their appearance again and again, followed by fantasy statements every time 'lover boy' made an appearance on the screen: 'Here I am,' she would say. And, 'I'll be your substitute whenever you need me.'

Then Jennifer Lopez appeared. Her sexy dance stance was appealing to Eldon's visual senses. His mind was filled with the thought of 'when will I dance with my lover again?' Now the naughty, yet emotional desperation pushed to the surface. 'Okay! You can park your shoes under my bed anytime.'

His eyes zoomed to wide angle, and from the right-hand corner of his eye, he could see her wrath. He also felt it. Her long, slender fingers curled snake like around her knees, and her fang-like nails bit into her kneecaps. Her feet tapped as if to music that she loved, and her face indicated an attack waiting to happen.

Alma surprised him with her attacking opening statement. As they left she said, 'Do you know how you made me feel inside there?'

'I feel like that all the time,' he defended. 'Have you heard yourself since we left home?'

'How dare you make me feel second-hand? How dare you!' she continued as if Eldon was not part of the discussion.

'Tell me, dearest, is it only your feeling we need to be concerned about?' he asked.

'How dare you? How dare you do that to me!' she said repeatedly all the way home. His knowledge about the tongue's faculty and function shockingly increased as he experienced firsthand how far-reaching its cutting edge delivered his individual outlook on life with of the finality of pruning shears. The sharpness of her tongue skilfully acted like an arrow, entering his ears and then finding its way to his heart by remote control. Then going for the kill, she released her final blow. 'This body of mine will be "out of bounds" until further notice,' Alma concluded.

'Okay, out of bounds. Does it matter? I have been living out of bounds already! Have I ever been allowed in? Guess not! Okay I already know my place; I've seldom moved from there! This dog handler had lots of coaching time with me. I'll just be fine.'

Later that evening, upon retiring, Alma's pressing emotions surfaced once again. 'Jenifer Lopez's name will never flow over your lips again!' she demanded.

Then, with a few words, Eldon made a closing statement: 'All of this just because I offered the sexiest actress a five-star parking spot for her shoes?'

After telling Jonathan the story, I asked, 'Will I stay in the relationship? Is it not similar to a woman returning to an abusive husband?'

Jonathan took his time to respond, 'Alwyn, when one can share his problem in such a manner as you just did, will he then not know the solution himself? Only he who lives his life can change his life.'

I nodded. 'Then I shall seek and find a new life-giving love'

Will pride, envy, and selfishness not becloud ones perceptive powers?
—*Wynie*

18

Like mother, like daughter

It was a Saturday, 6 September. The season of new life had just begun. Trees filled with blossoms bore evidence that there would be fruit in season. Boots were replaced by open shoes, and once again toenail polish called for attention. The song of the birds greeted the rising sun while they gathered food for their young. The call of Nature was all around.

The early sun warmed up the moods of everyone, or so it seemed. As I was about to enjoy my lunch break at my practice, I looked out of the window onto the driveway. A new Benz pulled in. A woman emerged from the car; her walk did not represent spring. She carried autumn with her as if wanting to exchange it for winter.

She just sat there in reception. She closed her eyes and did not wake up to the friendly 'Good day to you,' . She was then left to sleep, for it was evident that the exhaustion of crying has taken its toll. Lunch came to a close when she opened her blue-green eyes.

'How long have I been sitting here?' she asked with concern. 'I do not have an appointment. I'd like one now please, please.'

'Please come in,' I suggested. 'You seem exhausted?'

Her eyes were downcast, and her head was hanging as low as possible. To lift it up required great effort from her. 'Yes,' she said, like the pauper who did not dare to look the king in the eye.

'What brings you here, madam, and how can I assist you?'

'I am hurting all over and do not know were to start,' she said and lifted up her eyes. Their color shading was in need of a spark. I wondered when last they had sparkled.

'The beginning may be a good place to start,' I suggested.

'I don't feel like doing anything. My muscles are always hurting.'

'Always? How long has always been?' I probed.

'Since my father left my mother. I was thirteen years old at the time. Or it may have been at conception.'

I looked at her, awaiting more information. She looked at me as if I told her something she had already known. She did not offer a word.

'Mother, father, thirteen, and conception?' I hesitantly asked.

'My own husband walked out on me last week. Took only a few things. He left in a hurry. He left a note in the kitchen.' She retrieved the note from her bag and read aloud:

> Doll, this is the last time I will ever use your kitchen again. Today I am not cleaning up. Sorry, but I have a busy schedule, and you do have the privilege of a full-time maid. All will remain the same regarding the house, your lifestyle, your Benz. The lawyer has instructions to be fair and to file for divorce. I have never lied to you regarding my feelings for you and my concern towards you. I did not pretend to be the man I am not. You always stopped me whenever I discussed an issue I have. There is no other woman involved, and I know you will not believe me as usual. Quite frankly I do not expect you to believe me— you never did.

She stopped. With tears, anger, and sighing, she closed her eyes. 'Doc, now I know how my mother felt, or rather I believed so all the years, until yesterday. Yesterday at mom's place was just as shocking as reading this note for the first time there in my kitchen.' She broke the silence while opening her eyes.

Suddenly she demanded, 'Tell me, why did he walk out on me. Why?'

'Your husband or your father?' I probed

'Husband.'

'What did you discover yesterday?

'My father left a note as well. He could not take it anymore. He gave my mom a new name. He called her "Expect-a" in his note to my mother.'

'Expect-a?' I asked, wondering.

'She expected everything her way. He had to respect her way. She pulled her father's note from her bag and read:

> My expectations were not met, only yours. Your false behaviour at social gatherings at home and among others we knew encouraged everyone to adore you, for your dreams and desires met their expectation levels. Everyone respected you. I had to pretend for your sake that our marriage was perfect. I had to be the model of the human race.
>
> I had to live two lives; one on the inside of the door and the other outside. The outside life killed 'who' I am; the inside life reminded me of 'what' I am. I am not your 'go for that' and we 'must that' executer. I am a man, and will not return to your 'make believe' world of showing and impressing in order to be adored by those who love entertainment. I will now hunt for a woman who will share life with me. We will entertain one another, adore each other, and if those among us like what they see, let it be.

She lifted her hands to the ceiling. 'Like mother, like daughter. I'm screwed.'

I could not hold back. 'Why did you refer to conception?'

'I did? Did I?' She was obviously trying to remember what she had said.

'You did, didn't you?'

'O my, I did. I guess I did. What made me say it?'

There was silence for a long time. We heard a child playing just on the other side of the door. Then the woman spoke again. 'I was my mother's "meal ticket" and the guarantee that Dad would maintain her living standards,' she said. 'I just expected to have the same and be treated the same. I never felt welcome in this world for some reason unknown to me. But what I do know is that I was reminded often to not worry about children, for they only limit you in what you want.' She banged her fist on the table. The child on the other side of the door then started crying.

'I am ashamed. I need to change it.' She stood up and just walked out.

I did not see her for a year or more. Summer had me wanting fruit of the season, so desire had me enter a fresh food store. Behind a trolley, I was selecting fruit. As I stood with a melon in hand contemplating its freshness and ripeness, a hand tapped my shoulder.

'How are you?' she asked.

'You just walked out the last time I saw you so long ago,' I said. 'I have been wondering how you have been doing.' I was surprised to see her.

'I'm doing fine,' she said. Then she turned to the man and the boy who were with her. 'Let me introduce you,' she said. 'This is my divorced husband and my son Nicko.' To her son she said, 'Sweetie, this is the "mind mechanic" I told you about.'

'Divorced, my backside!' Nicko replied. 'They sleep over a lot. Mom does not nag like she used to,' he went on.

'You have a loving mother, young man,' I declared, 'who made a mind shift not only for her sake, but for your sake as well, for she was in your shoes as a youngster.'

'Yes, she is cool now,' he quickly responded.

'You better remember that,' his father threatened, 'for I will be your constant reminder, son, that both your mother and I had a major attitude change for the better, and you need to follow suit, young man. Cool?'

I noticed the sparkle in her blue-green eyes as she looked up to him with a smile that said, 'I am grateful.'

We said goodbye and continued our shopping. I felt her eyes on me after a minute or two and looked at her. She spoke without sound; only those who can lip read would have understood her words: 'I'm happy. Thank you.' Anyone, however, would have seen her big thankful smile.

If only we could win the hearts of all who are brought in contact with us. Even thoughts close to us. —Wynie

19

It would be grace

At 'forty-something' I was unmarried and in the market for a meaningful relationship. My interest in hip-swaying, long hair, and absolute feminine characteristics had my attention on high alert.

At a public business venue, the blonde woman's subtle stare at my shoes was a dead giveaway. Something about me was interesting to her; was it only my shoes? I had to find out. By walking down the passage and back, I would get confirmation. Yes, she was interested—also well behaved and good looking. I knew we would meet again under similar circumstance. How exactly, I did not know.

It all started happening the following week. We were both surprised when we walked into the same hardware store. With hasty words and a slight stutter, she put her words into an illogical sequence: 'Hi! Anny is there . . . there . . . there at the tool section. We just need . . . there she is.' She directed her index finger to the tool section in order to deflect the personal discomfort she was feeling.

'Alwyn! Hello!' Annie said. 'Are you following us? What brings you here? Louise and I . . .' It was as if she was introducing Louise and me to one another. I had obviously been the object of discussion before this second meeting.

The three of us were standing in a triangle formation. I felt Louise's eyes x-ray my entire being. It felt like a teenager encounter. Then we looked at one another and noticed the mutual acceptance. I knew that she knew, and she knew that I knew, that we might become more than just a mere 'hello how are you' acquaintances for some time to come.

It was not long before our relationship became more up-font and personal. We had many visits over many cups of coffee. Our times together were good; her presence was always welcome. She was soft spoken, yet emotionally sharp and mentally clear, as well as inquisitive. She was a good thinker too. Her eyes were soft. She was attentive, and most of her conversation consisted of questions, but when she made a statement, it was in no uncertain terms.

I was happy and excited, yet stressed, about life's practicalities. Being together with Louise had a 'life giving' power that couldn't be imagined; it had to be experienced.

As I sat opposite her, we were in excellent discussion, then she interrupted and changed the subject: 'I'd love for my mom to meet you.'

'You want me to meet your mom? You sound serious.'

'I am. It would mean the world to me,' Louise said in a soft, firm tone.

'At forty-something, meeting a grown woman's mom should be an interesting experience.'

'Yes, I would appreciate it. I left home for boarding school at a young age. It was partly my own choice. Mother was concerned and wanted me to make the right decisions in life. The relationship between my children's father and my mother is good. I'd just like her blessing regarding the person I'm involved with.'

'Okay, let's do it,' I said bravely.

Our relationship was intensely close. One of us would contemplate a topic or incident, and the other would know about it. Our indivisible intuition communicated itself without the utterance of any word. As we sat in a garden, served with drinks and snacks, I realized Louise had something to get off her mind. 'Now come out with it. What is on your mind?' I insisted.

'It is wonderful to be in a relationship where we understand one another so well. At the same time I am scared. It is too good to be true. Is this for real, Alwyn? Sometimes I wonder if I deserve this. I would never have dreamed of experiencing what we have.'

This statement shocked me. All my life I had gone out of my way to maintain good relationships with people in my circle of life. I had done this even more so to the woman who would share my life. In addition, I had always avoided, if possible, those who had a negative influence and a hostile attitude.

Her words, 'It is too good to be true,' had me concerned, for if it is good, why question it? I lost myself in a whirlwind of logic and emotions. I was just catching up with myself again when she spoke again. 'My mother will be coming over next weekend. School holidays also give her a break, for she works at an old age home. Visiting with me also gives her a breather from a demanding husband.'

She kept silent for a while. Her eyes became glassy, and with a turn of the head she tried to hide the show of emotion. It was as if history, full of incidental pit stops, had focused her mind on a road less travelled due to potholes that turned into quicksand.

Maybe, just maybe, the wrong rescuer had saved her from life's sinking sand. From what I had picked up between the lines by now, I reasoned that she would have wanted a more stable relationship, for her mother's sake. I wondered if Louise would have liked her mother to confirm her own statement: 'I would never have dreamed of experiencing what we have.'

Yes, she had experienced life's ups and downs, yet she had no 'holier than thou' attitude,' and after blinking her eyes a few times she concluded, 'My mother is bold in giving good advice. It comes from her real-life experiences, and she gives it only out of concern for her children.'

Time flies while you are enjoying it, so the moment of meeting her mother was only moments away. It was to be in a tea garden at a large nursery full of plants, trees, and flowers, for it was the month of December.

It was the most beautiful garden—full of every plant imaginable that could turn a dull garden into a sanctuary of peace with a life-giving atmosphere.

Spring has passed, and the midsummer's warmth was living up to the emotions of the season, inspiring any sensitive person to be the gardener of his or her own life and maintain the beauty as much as could be permitted.

Her mother looked at me. Wonder was evident in her eyes. At that stage, I would not have minded having the gift of mindreading. She looked tough, and my thoughts directed me back to my childhood days, to a lady who had spent most of her life in a wheelchair. Mrs Muller had had to accept life 'as is', for she had no choice other than to raise her two sons on her own. They, like her, were bound by wheelchairs and crutches.

I liked Louise's mother. What you see is what you get. I could not detect 'pretence', and she seemed to have only one expectation. She was straightforward and said that she liked me.

At the lower end of this tea garden, a small play park was filled with children around the ages of three to four. It was someone's birthday, and many of the little guests had cupcakes in hand, and the enjoyment of these treats was evident on their cheeks and noses. Dashes of pink, brown, orange, and green icing were being removed from their faces by indulgent mothers and fathers. Little feet were covered in a variety of colours of shoes and sandals, and even those who were barefoot kept themselves busy with chasing the geese and chickens.

'Are you here, Alwyn?' This was my call to attention. Louise enjoyed her mother's presence, and her need for meaningful communication was all over her face. Now they had my undivided attention, and I moved the discussion to everything about 'Granny'—where she came from, her preferences, how young she was, food, and the work she so faithfully did.

Her work at an old age home, I guess, had her determined, and a statement she made shocked me, though I kept my composure. 'Alwyn, I often pray and ask God to *shorten my life*,' she said. There was a silence, an atmosphere of shock. 'I am serious,' she said when she saw my eyebrows lift.

'Are you sure you know what you're asking?' I had to know.

Louise was shocked. She held her breath as her eyes fixed on her mother. Her own question was evident without a sound.

'What do I have to live for, my child? A husband who needs permanent care, and I spend my days working to comfort those who are needy, incapable, and dependant.'

I had had a similar experience with a dying man a number of years ago. Dave had not wanted his family to pretend he would live another ten years. The doctor predicted he would last only months, or even weeks, and he knew that the end was near. He was not going to give heed to the expectations of his wife and children. Here again, someone was prepared to open up to me.

'Granny, you must be careful for what you ask. It could be granted to you . . . wouldn't you rather want to reconsider it?' I requested.

Granny dropped her shoulders to the point of emptying her lungs. It was as if she knew that reasoning would not enable Louise and I to understand her. She then reached for her cup, took a sip of her tea, and said, 'I am *not* going to be a burden to anyone, more so my children.' She turned to Louise. 'I have had enough of life's hard side. It hasn't turned for me, and if I get much older, I will be on the miserable receiving end of it all.'

Louise looked devastated. I understood that her feelings were too tangled up for her to figure out what the real message was. We struggled to redirect the discussion from this topic, but once again, it returned. 'It would be grace,' Granny said and got my attention once again.

'Grace!' I called out, having an idea what she was on about.

Without uncertainty she confirmed, 'It would be a *token of grace* towards me.'

'Is there any chance of getting you to change your mind?'

'No. I do not expect anyone to understand it,' she said in a firm, assertive style. Uncle Dave's words, 'they will maybe someday grasp,' entered my mind.

We changed the topic again, and I found Granny to be a lovely woman. One could only wonder what had to have happened in her life—to what extremes she had been subjected—in order to be so firm about her choice.

The visit was good otherwise, and I was glad to have met her. Then, as we walked out of the beautiful, colourful plant collection, she placed her hand on my shoulders, looked up at me, and smiled with approval. Her gesture was very welcome.

Then there was Christmas.

'She likes you!' Louise said as she handed her mother's gift to me.

It was a short-sleeved summer shirt. 'She is a lovely lady,' I told Louise. 'It seems as if there are no pretences in her approach to life. Again, I have met someone who does not live life on a stage in order to impress an audience. Shakespeare may have agreed with me.' That was my discovery.

It was evident that Louise loved her mother. Two days after Christmas she informed me, 'I am going to spend more time with my mom, okay? We are going to do the mother-daughter thing. We will be shopping and visiting, and she will want to know more about you.' She left that evening.

The next morning at 9.20, her text reached me informing me that they were leaving home. It wasn't much after that that she phoned. 'We had an accident . . . I am worried . . . my mother . . .' her voice disappeared, and our call was disconnected. I felt my heart in my stomach, then acid flowed over it. My heart did not know how to escape this onslaught. I then stood still, breathed deeply, closed my eyes and prayed: 'God, please intervene and give us power once again.' I then called Louise back; another woman answered and said, 'The paramedics are on their way. She seems to be fine.' It was just what I needed to hear. I jumped into my car and got to the scene within minutes.

Emergency services were there; I walked over to Louise and heard her voice. She was fighting the medics who were struggling to support her back and neck. Taking hold of her hand, I said, 'Hey, I am here,' and then there was a power that entered her arm and pulled her forward. It was just the opportunity they needed; the medics did what they had to do.

There had been an impact on her left ankle; indeed it was positioned at a ninety-degree angle. They attended to her in a very professional manner.

In the meantime, I noticed that Granny was not being attended to. I walked to her. I was shocked with the evidence that her expectations had been granted. I had mixed emotions, and my thoughts were tumultuous. *Do ones expectations in life determine one's life?* I thought. *Is one's choice so powerful, and the string of influence it has to those around us?*

I shed tears. How wonderful would it have been to resurrect that person back to life for her family's sake? Would their expectations be controversial to her expectation? What would the outcome be? Would one ever understand?

My attention redirected again . . .

The sirens marked the departure of the ambulance for the hospital. I arrived soon after the ambulance. I had to wait a matter of minutes, but they felt to me like hours. Then I received news that Louise's condition was stable. What a relief! My 'heart' regained its rightful place.

New Year's Eve made its appearance before we had a chance to realize how fast time had ticked off. Louise was still in hospital, and our loss ensured that a gray cloud hung over our anticipation as we looked forward to the New Year. Had expectations been influenced by chance, or by a wish granted?

As I entered the hospital grounds, my childhood experience paid me a visit for a few moments as Mr Lee's voice echoed: 'You must be calm, not put fight in mind. Fight makes you sick.' His voice reminded me that a calm attitude is good for the human spirit.

Like Joshua of old, even for this sinner, I had undertaken a New Year's midnight visitation to instil hope in Louise. Not a soul had me in sight as I walked into the hospital and through the ward to her bedside. Louise was standing up against the wall. 'My mom . . . my mom . . .' is all she got out.

'I know . . .' I swallowed my words and emotion, for that was all could I say.

'Now my life will never be the same . . .' Louise said with certainty.

From a distance, the joyful sound of the New Year celebration was prominent. It was a reminder that, in any event, life carries on. We stood in welcome silence, for no word would serve as remedy. Only our presence together confirmed 'You're not on your own.'

Expectation where is thy beginning? Where is thy end?

It all still baffles the mind: 'too good to be true'.

However our relationship's grace also had to end.

_____

Are not our thoughts and feelings encouraged and strengthened as we utter them? —Wynie

20

Needy expectation

'How can I help you?' I asked the patient.

'I may be beyond repair,' she started.

'Beyond repair . . . why?' I continued.

She looked at me and turned her head away. 'Let's not go there, Doc. I'm here because my nerves are shot.'

'Okay.'

My assessment took a while. 'An ulcer is developing, Mrs Nell,' I said and advised her to exercise regularly and follow prescribed nutritional changes.

'Fine, if I need to. Do I really need to? Will it help? Do you think with medication I will be okay? I mean . . .'

'You mean?'

'Do I need help, Doc?'

'Help?' My eyes questioned.

'I think I need a shrink,' she said with a shivering voice.

'How will a shrink affect your situation? How do you think that will benefit you?' I asked.

'Is there hope for me, Doc?'

'How can you not know that answer?' I dared. The room became so silent that I heard my own heart beating. She stood up and walked to the door and back. The sound of her shoes on the floor echoed for miles. I needed to say something. She walked back to her chair and picked up her bag.

'You're right,' she said, then got hold of her cell phone and entered a number. 'I don't know if Mary-Ann will talk to me. She knows my number.'

'Hello Mary-Ann, Vanessa here . . . fine and you?' She spoke and shook her head in disbelief.

'Mary-Ann, please, I need your forgiveness. It is haunting me . . . for stealing your husband. Will you forgive me?'

Vanessa's whole body exhibited paralysis suddenly. Only her right hand remained in place with the phone to her ear. 'Okay, I . . . will do so. You mean . . . next week? Okay, I will talk to Deon. Thanks.'

'She's fine with me. Anyway, she wanted to get rid of Deon. Did you hear that? Can it be true?'

'Wanted to get rid of him? Will you put me in the picture?' I asked.

Vanessa was smiling and had tears running down her face—happiness and sadness all at one time. She told me how poverty had made her desperate and forced her to turn to part-time prostitution with a few 'well-to-do' businessmen.

She lived in a one-room apartment in a complex close to a suburb where middle-class people would not even think of living. She would entertain men, work at her job, and make the living she wanted.

Vanessa wanted to end her extracurricular income activity. For some time she told the married men that she was tired of being the substitute for their incompetent wives. Being the sex lady for different men made her realize that she could give one man all the energy she currently provided for many. It was well into the second year of this lifestyle that she met Deon.

She cracked the door open one evening. There he stood—well dressed, clean shaven, good looking, and shy. Then she opened her door completely. 'What a man!' Her face expressed delight and joy. 'Wow!' she told me. 'You see, Doc, I just could not negotiate a sex service with him. I was going to fall for him. I told him he had to talk to his wife.'

He told her that she reminded him of the rejection he experienced with his wife.

'So, you got upset, Vanessa?' I probed. 'Were you mad at him?'

'I would not have taken it from the other two men. I told them that they were assholes—that's why they came to me.'

'Then why be different with "what a man"? What was your take on him?'

'He did not come to me because of sexual frustration only, and I had experienced a different frustration before seeing this man,' she justified.

I had to know. 'Vanessa, did you *pretend* you're someone that you're not?'

'Maybe they had a need and I was the actress. I *pretended*.'

'*Expectation*,' I interrupted.

'And Mary-Ann had the nerve to say that I did her a favour and that she was seeing some other man anyway. Call it what you want, Doc. I don't have verbal diarrhoea, but these are the facts.'

Deon did not demand, and Vanessa did not want to *pretend* anymore. One Saturday she asked him not to ignore her request and not lose her number. He left her place not understanding why she sounded like a counsellor. More than embarrassed, he felt like a fool.

Deon spoke to his wife that same evening. She stated that there was absolute nothing wrong with their sex life, and his expectations were too high. She would think about increasing it to twice a month. Disappointed and angry, he asked the wife not to do him any favours, but rather to be a wife and lover to him. His wife said she loved him but his *expectation*s were unreasonable. Deon then jumped into his twin cab and made the engine express his emotions.

The highway was now the battlefield of grinding teeth like tyre-to-tar friction. It was not raining, but his eyes needed wipers. Later he realized that he was heading to the countryside. Yes, he wanted to get away from it all.

Deon felt as if he was being imprisoned—in solitary confinement— and his wife was the warden. Crying, depressed, upset, and angry about his relationship, he lost track of time. This brought him to his relationship's dead end. He made up his mind. Even so, the engine did not get the supply of petrol it needed, and it refused to roll on.

The twin cab came to a halt. Deon found himself in 'no-man's-land'. He called his wife to help him; ten litres of fuel would get him to the next town. She would have nothing of his stupid, childlike behaviour. He called a friend, explained his situation, and had to wait a few hours. Emotionally he was in 'no-woman's-land', and for the first time Deon was at peace with himself. He was done . . . at the end of his road.

He walked into his big house. Everything was normal except for the fact that Mary-Ann was not in front of the TV as usual. At one in the morning, he entered the bedroom and found Mary-Ann asleep like a baby. At first, he did not want to wake her, but he knew that if he did not, he wouldn't say what he had to say the way he knew had to. Gently, he woke her up.

'You back?'

'I am, and I need to talk to you.'

'O no! Not again,' Mary-Ann complained.

'Never again will I bother you—not for discussion, attention, love, or sex.'

'What are you getting at, Deon?'

'This relationship is no more,' he gasped for words. 'I have had enough.'

'Okay! Are you filing for a divorce?'

'I will see my attorney on Monday,' he confirmed. And so, it was done.

Vanessa did not see Deon for a number of weeks. She told the other two men that her own disgust in herself was eating at her bones. Her extracurricular income was degrading, and it was here where it ended.

'It was difficult in a way to get Deon out of my mind. He was just one of those men who would not go to a prostitute. What made him knock at my door. What kept the wonder of him alive in me?'

Her 'day off' at work was going to be limited, for her budget now dictated a change in her lifestyle. Sitting at home was going to be boring or even depressing. Thank God her friend Sue phoned, and the two made a breakfast date.

She got dressed and got into her vehicle. As she was driving out of the complex, Sue phoned. She could not make their appointment; she had an emergency to sort out.

On her way with nowhere to go, Vanessa let her mind operate on autopilot. Unbidden thoughts entered her mind—would Deon ever contact her again? Tears of frustration made her stop. Thinking that she might only spend her day window-shopping, she dropped her head on the steering wheel. Vanessa now had her mind full of despairing thoughts.

Then a knock on the window made Vanessa return to the fact that she was in her car. Turning her head, she saw young concerned girl looking at her. 'Are you fine?'

'Just . . . just.' Vanessa attempted to smile.

'Please get out for some fresh air,' the young woman pleaded.

Vanessa got out of her car after the friendly request. There, a few meters in front of them, coming out of the centre, was Deon. She saw him while his attention was on some window, and fell back to her seat as paralysis of the legs placed her buttocks back on the seat of her car.

After the young lady's outcry of 'Oh no, someone help!' Vanessa realized that Deon's attention had been redirected to her. The friendly woman told him she thought Vanessa was not well and gave him a brief description of what she had observed and how she had managed to get Vanessa out of her car.

'Thank you so much, Bea. I will handle it from here on and see that she is attended to,' Deon replied.

Bea and Uncle Deon knew one another. 'Okay!' She left for college.

'Hello, Vanessa,' he said. She did not look up. 'Hello, Vanessa,' he repeated.

'I did not expect to bump into you. Hello Deon.'

'Are you fine?'

'No! A friend and I had a breakfast date, but it was cancelled. Now I am going home.'

'I am glad he cancelled. And you're not in a state to drive home. You just heard me promise Bea that I would take care of you.'

'Are you also well?' Vanessa continued.

'Only after I buy you breakfast,' he said, and he helped Vanessa out of her car, locked it, and escorted her to the coffee shop.

They enjoyed their reunion and laughed about how nervous he had been at their first encounter. Vanessa noted how their lives had changed in ten months. Deon asked her out for supper the following week. With much delight, she said yes!

Then a cloud of coincidences came over them. Mary-Ann appeared at their table and said that Vanessa was the cause of her divorce. She promised that she would see to it that Deon would be ruined bit by bit.

'If you are incapable of looking after this man,' said Vanessa, 'if you are irresponsible and neglect to service him, or if you do not have the means to love—indeed he is on the verge of loving bankruptcy—I suggest you find a man you can afford who requires low maintenance.' Vanessa could not hold back after her wonderful reunion had been interrupted.

'Doc, was I glad to see him again,' she told me. 'You cannot imagine. And the way he spoke and treated me was . . .'

I had to keep her talking, '. . . was?'

'I was treated with respect. He never spoke down to me as the 'service lady' of the night. Condemnation was nowhere to be found. He never made me feel like someone who sold her body.'

'Like someone that sold her body?' I asked to make sure that guilt was not eating at her soul.

'I am not proud of what I have done, and I don't justify any of my actions. At the time, with the manner in which Deon treated me, I pardoned myself.'

'You pardoned yourself?' My probing went on.

'As I told the other two men, I was disgusted in myself. I let them go. Letting go of them gave me a sense of freedom.'

I changed the subject. 'How long did it take for the two of you to talk about getting married?'

'About eighteen months—eighteen wonderful months.'

'Only eighteen wonderful months?' I was probing again.

'And, more than three years of marriage.'

'And you obviously don't regret it, do you?' I dared.

'No I don't! Not at all. Deon is one in a million. Best man I have ever come across or known.'

'But she wanted to get rid of Deon anyway.' I reminded her.

'That day in the coffee shop she blamed me! The bi . . .'

'And you are blaming yourself?' I asked. Then she went quiet for a while.

The emotions were evident on Vanessa's face. Her facial indications went from happy to sad. Her hands turned into aggressive fists. Her legs jumped up and down. Her eyes went red with fluttering eyelids, which were also wet. It was as if she was in a trance.

'Vanessa, can you not forgive your disgust in yourself?' After I asked this, tears rolled down her cheeks.

'I should do that someday, Doc'

'Some day? One day? Another day? Today? Why not?' I went on.

Vanessa left my office. Three weeks later, she walked in with Deon following behind her. She introduced Deon to me. After a while, he made a statement: 'Whatever happened in these rooms that day made my wife new in her approach to me and others. Can that really happen?'

'The only place where the changes happened was in her mind,' I told him. 'All I know is that Vanessa did not want to pretend anymore; neither did she want to live out the expectations of others.'

He looked at me and reached out to shake my hand. 'Something happened, and it makes me want to love her even more.'

They said goodbye.

Guilt, grief, and anxiety may not be remedied; but will hope, cheerfulness and gratitude not brighten our life path? —Wynie

21

Who will dare explain how they feel?

There was a beep as the text message arrived. Sunday morning at 1.25. I raised my eyelid just enough to recognize who the sender was. 'Okay, time to go.'

After a glass of lemon water, on my way out I collected my emergency kit. The text was from a mother in distress for her daughter, as she had been so many times before: 'Sammy is in a coma again. Will you help, please?'

Sammy was twenty-two years young and missing out on the normal 'life offerings' having been hijacked by physical underdevelopment since puberty. Motionless, Sammy was on her bed. I dropped medication in minute measures on her tongue at regular short intervals.

My eyes were drawn to the picture I had experienced many times in the past, only this time my memory took me back to that lonely ward where the frail Suzan's health deteriorated and I witnessed life's final moments.

'Her sugar measured very high,' Beatrice, Sammy's mother, informed me.

This mother's anxiety was evident; however, her shock was not that intense, for this was not the first time. Her face reflected a tiredness, and yet a message that she would not give up. Her hands suggested that she needed to do something, so I placed my order: 'Something hot to drink please?'

In the quiet morning hours, I could hear the water boiling in the distance. Eventually Sammy responded. Her eyes opened and then closed again, while a tear flowed from the corner and over her nose, stopped at the tip as if it hesitated to take the leap down to her cheek. Her hand moved to wipe the tears, then she spoke: 'Thank you, Uncle . . . I am thirsty . . .'

Beatrice returned and tested Sammy's sugar again. 'Just under four . . . I'll get her some Coke . . .' And she left the room for that black 'holy water'.

As I drove back home, my mind was locked in the duality of two young people. The short life history of each of them was a story that had a far-reaching influence on others around them. Suzan's parents had broken up; their relationship was no more after the loss of their daughter. Here was another broken relationship, notwithstanding the storm of a health issue.

By three fifteen I was back in bed. By five thirty I was up and showered, for the day's tasks lay ahead. Apples and grapes made an excellent breakfast with two hard-boiled eggs. The simple meal would supply energy after little sleep that night.

When I arrived at the office, there was a senior couple waiting in a friendly but anxious mood. 'Doc,' Mrs Van Eck said, 'we are here on serious business. Geriatrics or not, are you up to it?' Her request was hurried.

'I suggest we discuss it in my office and see if we may become any wiser,' I responded. They followed my gesturing hands and entered my office.

They sat on the edges of their chairs. I wondered, *Are they in a hurry?*

'We would like to get to the bottom of this as soon as possible, now would we not, darling?' she turned to her husband. It seemed that Mrs Van Eck, seventy-one years young, would do all the talking.

'Now then, how may I assist you?' I offered.

She did not give the question time to settle. 'You will be helping me by helping him.' She pointed to her husband.

Then I turned to the sixty-seven-year-young Mr Van Eck 'What would you like me to do for—'

She did not wait for his response to the question 'Doc, I need him to elevate all the way to the fiftieth floor. He goes only up to floor twenty-eight—or twenty-nine at times. Sometimes he reaches the fortieth floor.'

'Do you have a fear of heights . . . ?'

'Oh no, you do not understand . . .' And then they both blushed. Mr Van Eck placed his arms around his head as if protecting himself from severe blows to the head.

She threw yet another blow: 'Doc, I may be old, but I am far from cold. This woman needs her man to reach his full "length potential"! He is not old!'

'Okay! You want your hubby to stand up to the task,' I summed it up.

She noticed his discomfort, and out came her charm. 'Doc, all these years he has been like the vibrant ball player, fit and on the ball. All I am doing is looking after this wonderful asset of mine.' She hugged Mr Van Eck and kissed his hand.

I attended to them, and Mrs van Eck walked down the stairs with swinging hips and hair. One would say she had a teenager's 'swing' after she had accomplished her goal.

That Monday I looked forward to the moment when I would lock the day's work behind me. The last patient walked in, Mr Peacock.

'Doc, I have good news for you . . . you do not need to be worried about my surgery. The specialist said my heart will be fine, and your concern was unfounded,' he explained.

'Uncle Peacock, do you really need this knee replacement . . .'

He was quick in responding 'Everyone around me says that I will only benefit from it, and the specialist assures me that it will be for the better. My family all want the best for me.'

I had discovered something in life—it is not easy to change a human's mind once it is made up, especially when the odds weigh heavily in favour of a desired outcome.

In order to maintain Uncle Peacock's positive attitude, I responded in kind: 'Well, I am glad the specialist's finding is positive. Then you will do well.'

'Thank you, Doc. I will be in the theatre on Friday . . . I must go now, if you will excuse me,' and he left with hope that overflowed.

I sat with my face in my hands. 'O, God, please let this operation be successful . . .'

The week went by with the speed of light, and it was Friday again. Sammy's mother was not doing well, and I decided to visit their home. On my arrival, I encountered a fragile atmosphere. Sammy's younger sibling and her mother, Beatrice, were more than unhappy with one another. The mother's endurance was wanting. She was exhausted and irritated. Except for Sammy, Beatrice's family were insensitive to this mother's sacrifice.

Mother was in 'consultation' with the demanding teenage sibling, and I placed myself on a big couch. Sammy seemed exhausted as she came out from the kitchen, walked closer, and greeted me. Her face was lifeless, her legs were dragging her body along, and her eyes were full of tears.

'May I sit next to you?' Her mouth hung, and her eyes floated with a directionless stare, yet a power of some kind kept her head up.

'Of course you may,' I invited

'I am tired . . . very tired . . .' She sighed, then no more words followed.

'Tired of . . .' I probed as I looked at Sammy out of the corner of my eye. This was not light complaining and indulging in self-pity; this was a serious discussion starting.

'I do not want this anymore,' she said. 'All this is because of me.'

'Because of you?'

'I am tired of being like this.' A disgusted expression confirmed the statement. 'All this is because of me,' she said yet again.

Turning to her, I asked, 'Sammy, are they at one another because of you?'

'I am a burden in their lives. They do not say it. However, it is obvious,' she continued as if she had not heard me.

'They love you . . . care for you . . .'

'You think I do not know that, Uncle ? I am very aware of that. I am holding on only for my mother's sake.'

'Only hold on?'

'Onto life . . .' The tone of her voice had me very concerned, for her words flowed out with the sounds of life's final breath.

I recalled Uncle Dave, and I recalled Granny saying that a shortened life 'would be grace'. These thoughts had me wondering about what Sammy was getting at. 'Holding on to life for your mother's sake? What about for Sammy's sake?' She must have heard the pleading in my voice.

Sammy looked up and then closed her eyes. Her lips compressed, as if containing a sound that was not to be voiced. She shook her head. 'For me, I want it to end,' she said. 'I suffer. I do not have a normal life. I am tired of clinging onto everyone around me for dear life. I am a woman, yet I am not.'

'What do you want . . . for yourself?' I was hoping I could implant some positive thinking.

'My school friends have all grown up. I do not blame them for not visiting me. I understand. They have normal lives. I am their age, but I have not grown. In fact, my life is . . .' She stared off into the distance. 'What do I want? I love my mother . . .' And her tears flowed freely then. 'I do not want to hold on anymore.'

'You are sure of this, Sammy?' I felt I needed to control my emotions.

She turned to me, her eyes red and pleading for me to understand. 'Is it wrong of me?'

I could only shake my head, and only after a few seconds did I realize what I had indicated. 'We all make very important decisions in our lives, especially when we are in a desperate state of need. Who other than you can make that choice? You must make the choice for yourself.'

She sat back and lifted her hips to relieve the pressure. 'I don't want to hang in there any more,' she whispered.

Then silence filled the lounge. We looked at one another, knowing what the likely outcome of our discussion would be. I nodded, she nodded, and we understood our conclusion. Sammy said goodbye and went to bed. Our tears were evident.

The home was quiet and peaceful after a while. Beatrice and I had discussion full of meaningful content. It allowed the stress release valve to open, and she expressed her deepest feelings. Her eyes were more at peace, the anxiety in her voice calmed down, and she seemed fine for the moment.

Later, after I had returned home, my mobile rang a bit after eight o'clock. It was Uncle Peacock's daughter. 'I just wanted to inform you that the surgery was a success,' she told me. 'Dad's in ICU for now.' She kept her news short and concise.

'I am happy to hear that,' I told her sincerely. 'Thanks for letting me know.' I felt happy, and heaved a sigh of relieve.

On Saturday morning I enjoyed breakfast. It was my day off, and my previous evening's chat with Sammy was still vividly echoing through my mind. My mobile rang for the first time that day; it was seven thirty. The call was from Uncle Peacock's son-in-law. 'We have bad news,' he said. 'My wife's father passed away in the early hours of the morning. It was cardiac arrest.' He struggled to get the message out.

'I . . . I am sorry to hear that,' I told him. 'Please give the family my . . .' I was shocked. I got into my car and drove a distance. I then hunted for a solitary spot where I could be still.

First, an old woman who was not cold but needed her expectations to be provided. Second, a man caught between two directions because others around him had different expectations for him. Third, a twenty-two year old woman who did not want to suffer any more. *How controversial were their expectations and desires?*

I then wondered, *The chord between life and death, how fragile it is, yet how powerful it is, and who will alter it?*

I found myself in a big shopping centre; the windows displayed various products. Promotional and marketing strategies were drawing the attention of people walking by who admired and desired the items that were for sale.

We may pay the price for our choice of clothing, shoes, food, and entertainment, and we may get what we expect. But what price tag will we put on life's expectations?

Ten meters ahead, I saw Mrs And Mr Van Eck walking hand in hand. Her hips were swaying, and there was a spring in her step. She was dressed almost like a teenager, and she pulled her man to a window that displayed gold and shining stones—because diamonds are a woman's best friend. I could see that it seemed obvious to her that a second diamond was required to represent their current bliss. She dragged him into the store. I watched as she selected rings to try on.

Two weeks went by. Beatrice called to inform me that Sammy was in hospital. 'She is not well. We are very concerned. Her doctor said they are doing the best they possibly can.' She conveyed the message as she had done so many times before, with expectation that Sammy would come home again.

In my mind, again, I saw Sammy looking up and closing her eyes, her lips compressed, as if containing a sound she did not want to release. This had my heart in my throat, for it reminded me of the conclusion of our discussion.

The following week, Sammy's family received the bad news that no mother and father ever want to hear. The expectation of all parents is that their children should outlive them, but this was not to be with Sammy. Who would dare explain how they felt? Who would dare describe their pain?

At the memorial service, in the midst of the music and song, again I heard her cry 'I don't want to hang in there anymore!' and the controversial expectations in human experience reminded me about the 'wonder' of life.

The next day Mr and Mrs van Eck were just in time for their appointment. They were there to pick up their grandchild.

'Doc, this is the family's baby,' Granny proudly said.

'I'm not a baby! I am big,' the child reminded her grandmother. 'I go to school!'

Here was a child who wanted to be big; there was Sammy who wanted to be a grown adult woman. I wondered once again about my personal loss of a love's connection. Could I have had the privilege of a life journey that may have extended to generations to come? What about my expectation had been wrong?

Turning to the young girl, I asked, 'How old are you?'

She showed me with fingers held high. 'Four!' she sang with confidence.

Granny interrupted 'Doc, we are doing well. I feel young again.' She smiled at Mr van Eck.

'Granny, you're *old*!' A harsh reminder echoed though the room.

That statement did not faze the seventy-one-year-young granny. 'Doc, we are so happy. We've even decided to renew our vows—before the second honeymoon!' she said with a naughty expression on her face.

Many want to be older, yet others need to be younger. Is this an age-old phenomenon?

As they left, Mr van Eck turned back. 'I have no other complaint but for one,' he whispered. 'This is an expensive exercise . . . or shall say expectation!'

'Mr van Eck, what is your expectation?' I asked. I needed to know.

He responded with a statement that sounded like an eco of my own thoughts. It was as if he had read my mind. He reminded me of my own discovery: 'Doc, in the past my expectations mostly made my life and those around me miserable. My expectations for my tomorrows have no secure grounds. Today is a wonderful gift; I dare not neglect it . . . I live it.'

I could only smile; my face confirmed my agreement.

Mr van Eck lifted his shoulders and followed his wife, as a willing teen would do.

Is a human not vulnerable? Why does he have the idea of being untouchable?
—Wynie

About the Author

Alwyn was a young boy in Johannesburg at age six where, he believes, his observation and study of human beings had its origin.

The suburb of Mayfair and surroundings represented all the nations of the world to him. Portuguese, Lebanese, Greek, Italian, Japanese, Chinese, German, British, Indian, Dutch, and Israeli. Black and white Africans—all of them had and made an impression of some kind. The way they lived and, most of all, what they spoke about.

Being in their homes, businesses, and under their noses was a discovering experience among the best.

Alwyn needed to experience "agreement" among humans. Pretence, in his mind, would be a repelling act among people, even from the age of six.

His ability to pay close attention and observe the behavior of those he mingled with had him in many uncomfortable positions and controversial situations.

In his midthirties, he turned from engineering to alternative medicine and life coaching. The hunt for mutual agreement continued, a commodity that is scarce within relationships of all kinds.

His practice provided a platform for many of those he treated that shared their real-life challenges. His discoveries were many as he worked with parents that had lost their children, those with relationship concerns, and those that found a new hope and outlook to life.

Alwyn believes that real-life events or challenges is the tutor without a face. That tutor that earns respect—he is no respecter of any person. The syllabus of life isn't formulated by any human being.

With gratitude, he looks back at a discovering journey where one learns about people among people.